KNOWING
YOUR
VALUE

KNOWING YOUR VALUE

*Women, Money, and Getting
What You're Worth*

Mika Brzezinski

WEINSTEIN
BOOKS

The survey mentioned in the introduction was conducted online within the United States by Harris Interactive on behalf of MSNBC from August 25th–27th, 2010 among 2,273 adults ages 18 and older. This online survey is not based on a probability sample and therefore no estimate of theoretical sampling error can be calculated. For complete survey methodology, including weighting variables, please contact www.harrisinteractive.com.

ISBN: 978-1-60286-134-3 (hardcover)
ISBN: 978-1-60286-160-2 (paperback)
ISBN: 978-1-60286-142-8 (e-book)

First Edition 2011
First Paperback Edition 2012

10 9 8 7 6 5

For my girls,
Emilie and Carlie.

May you always know your value.
All my love,
your crazy Mommy

CONTENTS

Acknowledgments   *ix*

INTRODUCTION
Success and Failure, All at Once   *1*

CHAPTER 1
My Story: How It Begins   *11*

CHAPTER 2
Get Out of Your Way: Women as
Their Own Worst Enemies   *31*

CHAPTER 3
What's a Woman Worth? The Gender Wage Gap
and the Perception of Value   *51*

CHAPTER 4
Acceptable Behavior: A Cautionary Tale about
Women Acting Like Men in the Workplace   *73*

CHAPTER 5
What Men Know: We Can't Act Like Them,
but We Can Learn from Them   *95*

Contents

CHAPTER 6

At the Bargaining Table:
Table Manners and Tactical Maneuvers *115*

CHAPTER 7

Allies and Enemies: A New Appreciation of Men
in the Workplace, and a Warning About Women *139*

CHAPTER 8

Motherhood: The Game Changer *157*

CONCLUSION

My Story: How It Ends—for Now *179*

Index *187*

ACKNOWLEDGMENTS

First, a heartfelt thank-you to the extraordinary women (and men) whom I interviewed for sharing their invaluable time and insights with me.

I'd like to thank Janet Klein for being my writing partner on this book, for collaborating on the entire concept and content. This project was exactly what we needed as women who struggle to know our value.

Putting it together has been a learning experience for everyone involved. Special thanks to Amanda Murray, Dana Haller, and Lauren Skowronski for their editorial assistance in getting this project to the finish line. You are amazing women, and the world will know your value only if you tell it. Don't hold back.

To Mel Berger and Judy Hottensen, this has been the most joyful challenge. Thank you for getting behind me once again.

My deepest gratitude and appreciation to my husband for putting up with me every day. This is an understatement. Jim, you have the patience of a saint, and the girls are lucky to have you as their father and mentor.

And now for the two biggest reasons I wrote this book: my girls. I thank my daughters for inspiring me every day to share this message with other women. Emilie and Carlie, I want the sky to be the limit for both of you in life. Know your value. Mommy truly does.

KNOWING YOUR VALUE

Success and Failure, All at Once

FEBRUARY 2008

Joe Scarborough sat across from me in the windowed café at the bottom of Rockefeller Center. Outside, the rink was filled with bundled-up skaters enjoying the winter chill. Joe and I, along with the rest of the *Morning Joe* staff, had just returned from a grueling three-week cross-country trek covering the historic 2008 presidential primaries. It was an exhilarating time to be working on a political talk show.

After months of hard work, *Morning Joe* was becoming the place for candidates to be seen and heard. The buzz was growing, our ratings were improving, and the show was making news. We should have been ecstatic. Instead Joe sat silently and listened as I explained why I needed to resign.

It was a painful decision. But after nearly twenty years of scrambling up, down, and back up the television-news ladder several times over, I was done. I was demoralized—and not because I didn't like my job. In fact, I loved it. No other show I'd ever worked on had such energy and so much excitement. But as I explained to Joe on that sad, cold winter morning, I could no longer work for a network that refused to recognize my value. It may have taken me forty years, but I'd finally realized it was time to do things right or not at all.

Despite my professional experience, the fifteen-hour workdays, and a successful new show that I had helped build, MSNBC was still refusing to pay me what I was worth. Not only was my salary lower than my colleagues', each month was a financial scramble to make ends meet. After child care, on-air wardrobe, makeup, travel, and the other ridiculous expenses that women in this business end up taking on, the job was actually costing me more than I was being paid. Checks were bouncing, and worse, I could barely face myself in the mirror when I thought of the example I was setting for my twelve- and fourteen-year-old daughters. Every morning I sat with a group of male colleagues, all of whom made much more than I did. In fact, our salaries weren't even close.

Let me be clear: there is no question that Joe was worth more to the show's success than anyone. But was he really fourteen times more valuable than me?

To be fair, Joe and I started out at *Morning Joe* on very different footing. The show was Joe's creation, and his sheer determination got it on the air. He had been hosting his own prime time talk show at the network, and his salary was on par with other prime time hosts. MSNBC was in the middle of a massive financial restructuring, making difficult staff cuts in an effort to keep the network productive during tough times.

When Joe recruited me as his cohost, I had been doing a low-level, part-time job at MSNBC, just to get back in the game after losing my anchor position at *CBS Evening News* the year before. I had worked my tail off to help *Morning Joe* become the success it was, and my career was again on the upswing—so really, why was I jeopardizing it? Because I was not getting paid my value. And because ultimately I had only myself to blame.

I sat across from Joe over breakfast to tell him that I had reached the breaking point. I owed it to Joe to tell him in person and to thank him for his heroic efforts to revive my career. But the inequity was killing me, and I believed it would ultimately poison the show. I was ready to walk away.

Before I could finish, he said, "No, you can't leave."

Joe knew I wasn't being paid what I was worth and had been fighting for me all along, but so far his efforts had been in vain. He asked for a few more days. As always, Joe had a plan.

The former congressman knew we had created something that was unlike anything else on television; how the on-air chemistry among Joe, myself, and Willie Geist was just right; how our lively debates were making waves and grabbing the attention of policy makers, politicians, and the media. Joe knew that as much as anyone, I was responsible for our on-air success. He had told anyone who would listen that his

3

vision for his new show would succeed only if I were his co-host. He was as angry at the NBC brass as I was. But what made matters worse was that I—me, myself—was to blame for this. I had allowed this to happen. I had asked repeatedly for a raise, but I had repeatedly been denied. The truth is, like most women, I didn't know my value, and even if I had, I wouldn't have known how to get it.

Looking back, I realize that every time I sat at the nego-tiating table, my greatest enemy was myself. The words I chose and the strategies I put in play actually undermined my goals. No manager and no network executive was responsi-ble for my plight. The failure to effectively communicate rested solely on me, every time.

My meeting with Joe that February morning was the cul-mination of a problem that had been brewing for decades. I had spent my career moving from job to job, accepting pay that I knew wasn't competitive because I always felt lucky to be there. I figured if I just worked hard, took on more hours, more assignments, and more stories, I could prove myself, and eventually my bosses would reward me with a raise and promotion. Often while I was hustling and hoping for more money, I would discover that my male colleagues were mak-ing more than I was. I wouldn't get angry at the men for this—I'd be angry at myself for not earning more respect (and compensation) from management. Then I'd start feeling un-derappreciated, talk to other networks, and then move on and repeat the pattern somewhere else. Clearly the pattern wasn't getting me anywhere.

Why was I continually underpaid and undervalued? Was

it because I was a woman? No. There are women in this business who rake in huge salaries. Like me, they are commodities. But these women know their value, and they get it. So what were they doing that I wasn't?

I had spent months watching Joe get what he wanted from management with ease and determination. I, too, was capable of doing great things for the show, but when it came to fighting for myself, I always struck out. I began asking myself whether I was the biggest idiot on the face of the earth. Here I was, playing the role of a strong, successful woman on the set who takes on the political hotshots and keeps the guys in check. And yet my salary was where it might have been fifteen years ago, or twenty years ago. This wasn't where I should have been at my age and level of experience.

I started to think about what was keeping me back, and what was keeping all women back. I kept seeing headlines about how far women have come. They have broken glass ceilings. Hillary Clinton has run for president. And yet women's salaries still don't equal men's salaries—women everywhere still make less.

I thought to myself, "Is it possible? Is it possible that I'm not alone? Have other successful women had some of the same problems? Or *am* I alone?" I started talking to the incredibly impressive women on the set, and they all told me, "Oh, no, no. You're not alone." One of these women actually came to me for advice when she was changing jobs, and I realized she was doing the same thing I was. Undermining herself. Undercutting herself. Undervaluing herself.

And then about a year ago, on a beautiful spring day, I was in the White House and dropped by presidential adviser Valerie Jarrett's office to say hello. We started talking about work-life balance. We discussed the excitement and challenges of having so many opportunities as women. For Valerie, the challenges were raising an incredible daughter on her own, navigating the worlds of business and politics at the top level, and helping to propel the first African-American president into office. For me, they were trying to maintain a marriage, raising two extraordinary girls while traveling the country, and covering the Obama presidency.

We marveled at all that was possible but also commiserated about the cost of our choices. The sacrifice. The determination that meeting our challenges required. I had just written a memoir, and I mentioned that I had an idea for another book, but I didn't think my schedule would allow me to write it. I wasn't getting enough time with my family. I could barely do any of my jobs well. I was wavering about whether this was a project I should throw myself into.

She asked what the concept was, and as I described to her my theories about women and value, I realized immediately I'd hit a nerve. She said, "You have to write this book. This is important. This is the next part of the conversation. Even more, this book is in you. You have to write it. It's *so* important." And then she proceeded to tell me about the White House Council on Women and Girls, and its efforts for National Equal Pay Day, the Lilly Ledbetter Fair Pay Act, the Paycheck Fairness Act, and all the studies they had underway. She told me the administration had people at every level dealing with women's issues, whether it be access to capital or the gender wage gap. Valerie not only urged me to write the book, she said, "I'll help you. What can I do? We've gotten really far. Women run the world. But we're not getting our value."

She was an inspiration to me and a catalyst for this project. What really was just a casual visit had taken a dramatic turn, and I walked out of her office knowing I was going to write this book. I realized that if my story spoke to Valerie, then certainly it would speak to others.

Luckily, *Morning Joe* is a place where power players come to be a part of the national conversation. So I didn't have to go too far to find successful women who were willing to be interviewed on the subject of knowing their value. I spoke with influential women in government such as Brooksley Born, Sheila Bair, and Elizabeth Warren; personal-finance expert Suze Orman; media entrepreneurs Arianna Huffington and Tina Brown; women's magazine leaders like *More* magazine's Lesley Jane Seymour and *Cosmopolitan*'s Kate White. I interviewed Nora Ephron, Joy Behar, and Susie Essman. I spoke to top researchers on the subject of gender and negotiation, such as Harvard's Hannah Riley Bowles. For the male perspective, I asked the likes of Donald Trump, Jack Welch, and Donny Deutsch to weigh in. Some of the interviewees had been on the show; some, like Facebook COO Sheryl Sandberg and Yahoo CEO Carol Bartz, I thought *should* be on the show.

The women I interviewed manage multibillion-dollar companies, run our government, and oversee our economy. These are women who deal day to day with challenges of national importance, yet I was struck by how similar our psychology was as we shared our experiences in the workplace. I assumed such successful women must somehow have been smarter about their careers and their money. They must have taken a different road—we couldn't possibly have made similar mistakes. But as I began sharing my struggles with women in a variety of fields, many of them told me of their own troubled efforts to get a raise, earn a promotion, or just to have their ideas heard in the conference room. Why are things that seem to be simple for many men so difficult for many women? Why do we undermine ourselves, often right from the start?

There are lessons to be learned from my experience, and from the experiences of a number of far more successful women I spoke with when writing this book.

How have they managed to be compensated for their true value? What have they done wrong, and what have they done *right*? Their answers were surprisingly honest and unexpectedly revealing. Apparently none of them played the game exactly the way the men did. Among other things, they taught me some important lessons about getting out of my own way, learning to speak up, negotiating from a place of power instead of fear, owning my success, and perhaps most important, getting the compensation I deserve.

After all, there's money to be made in these lessons. And the lessons apply to everything in life. Money, in this book, is simply a metaphor. This is about being valued in the way you should be at work or anywhere. Every lesson that you will read about in this book can apply to relationships, raising children, marriage, being in a profession, being in an industry, changing jobs . . . everything. Because if you don't demand what you're worth and if you don't communicate it well, you won't be treated fairly, and the relationship will ultimately die. And if you don't ask for what you deserve, you won't ever find out what you're made of, and what you truly can do. You undermine yourself by not developing your tools and learning what to do with them and what not to do with them; how to use your voice, your brain, your words, your style, your approach, your finesse, everything in your power to get your value.

It's okay to say what you want and what you need. Because if you want a relationship to work, you've got to get what you want and what you need. If you don't, you're giving, giving, giving, and you end up with nothing. Absolutely nothing.

Ultimately, MSNBC showed me the money. I got a significant raise, but not in the way I would ever have anticipated. Mine truly was an unconventional path, and I advise you not to walk it yourself. I'll tell you more about my experience later in the book.

To its credit, MSNBC not only made good, but it has taken up the cause. After I got this book contract I went to our boss, Phil Griffin—one of the stars in this book and the man who passed on giving me a raise until I was able to effectively communicate my value. I said to him, "Listen, I've got a book deal. I'm going to write about knowing my value, and I'm going to write about the mistakes I've made. And I want to write about mistakes I've made with you." He thought about it for less than a second and said, "Absolutely."

Then Phil raised the bar and suggested we go further. We started talking about ways we could feature the issue on the show, and MSNBC even did an online survey to provide research for the book (for details on methodology, see the copyright page). Even after reading the manuscript of this book, Phil has been on board as my biggest cheerleader. He knows a story that will resonate and, yes, sell. After all, the issue of equal pay, the gender wage gap, knowing your value—these are perennially important issues that affect women everywhere. And in the current "man-cession," as men are losing their jobs and families are depending more heavily on women's income, equal pay is an issue that's more timely than ever, and truly affects everyone.

There are a variety of reasons for gender inequality in the workplace. Many of them are complicated, and some are not completely understood. But in sharing these cautionary tales and personal victories, research and anecdotal evidence, I hope women will learn something that helps them chart their own course. I don't claim that we will eliminate the gender wage gap—not even close. But we can strategize and do much better for ourselves, and for the next generation. What I've learned from the women I've interviewed will stay with me. I want to share their wisdom with my daughters, and in this book I will share their wisdom with you.

CHAPTER 1

MY STORY
How It Begins

REBUILDING MY CAREER, BUT NOT MY VALUE

When I started at MSNBC in 2007, I was really starting over.

At the time, I had been out of work for almost a year after losing my job as a weekend anchor and a *60 Minutes* contributor at CBS News. In the wake of a scandal about a *60 Minutes* story on George Bush's military record and a management shake-up, I was let go with hardly any notice and little financial cushion.

I spent the year that followed searching for a job with the help of an agent who arranged meetings for me with executives at the various broadcast and cable networks. Every month, my prospects went down a rung. First, my agent was able to set up meetings with network presidents. Then I was meeting with vice presidents, then talent recruiters. Before long, I could barely get an appointment with anyone. I was nearly forty years old, and my career was in shambles—basically I was old news. My best days appeared to be behind me, and I wasn't considered a worthy investment.

After months of fruitless searching, I realized the right strategy was to start over. I had worked at NBC's cable division earlier in my career, and I had liked it there. The people knew me, and it had been a good fit. So I called MSNBC and begged for a job. Not a job they thought I would take given my experience, not a job they thought I would want, but whatever on-air job they had available. Reluctantly, the president of NBC News told me there was an opening for a news-reader position: someone who would read thirty-second news updates, called cut-ins, three times a night on MSNBC. He was describing a low-paying freelance position, and I grabbed onto it for dear life, like a ledge that I hoped would stop the free fall of my career.

If you looked at that MSNBC job in the context of my resume, you'd see that it was a considerable step back from my high-profile correspondent job at CBS. It was even a big step back from my job at MSNBC ten years earlier. I spent my fortieth birthday doing cut-ins, but it was fine. It was work, and I was proud of myself. My girls were watching Mommy take a huge step back in order to bring home a paycheck. There was as much value in this moment as the day I got a huge contract at CBS that included a *60 Minutes* deal. I was going to be okay. We were going to be okay.

After a year of having their mother home and with money being tight, my two daughters were ready for me to go back to work. My husband, Jim, definitely was. They were all used to me as a working mom, and they knew I enjoyed it. Work was what made me sparkle, and it was what I contributed to the household. I earned money far better than I cooked dinner. The job reading news cut-ins would be a piece of cake, and a part-time position was better than no position. I had to be realistic about my current value in the marketplace.

While I have regrets about not knowing what my compensation could and should have been at key moments in my career, I look back at the decision to take that job with great pride. Part of knowing your value is knowing when it is down and when it's time to take steps to rebuild. My biggest challenge has been knowing when my stock is up.

My first months back at MSNBC, I worked about four hours each day. In between my thirty-second news cut-ins, I paid my bills and listened over the phone to my girls' piano practice. After a year of unemployment, this job was just fine. It was predictable, it was good for the kids, and it was great to be back in the game, but the work was boring. Extremely boring. I felt confident of my talent, but I couldn't do much with it in that position.

It wasn't long before the executive producer of daytime-news programming recruited me to substitute host full news hours during the day. Within weeks I was on the schedule for the cut-ins as well as the full hour at three PM on weekdays. MSNBC and NBC started to give me assignments throughout the building, and my days became more interesting and a lot longer.

My hosting duties weren't as high profile as the role I had played at MSNBC seven years earlier when I cohosted the women's show *HomePage* with Ashleigh Banfield and Gina Gaston. Nor was it on the level of my lead role covering the 2000 presidential election and recount. But it was a job in the field I love.

After my first time substituting on a news hour, the word spread quickly about my performance; my new colleagues, who knew nothing of my long history in the business, were coming up to me in the halls, giving me high-fives and saying, "Wow! You're really good!"

In this business, you are as good as your last story. On cable, apparently you are as good as your last on-air minute.

I was tapped to do an *NBC News Special Report* when Brian Williams was unavailable and no one else was around. My delivery was flawless, and once again everyone seemed pleasantly surprised. No one remembered or had any idea that I did dozens of special reports for CBS News. So here I was, suddenly an up-and-comer all over again.

Still, I smiled and accepted the compliments. I was grateful for the opportunity to show the producers what I could do. The network realized I was useful, and I was convinced that sooner or later the right job would open up for me. Three months later, it did.

In May 2007, Don Imus was pulled off the air for making offensive statements about the Rutgers women's basketball players during his early morning show. Immediately there was a three-hour void on the MSNBC airwaves. I remember thinking, "Oh god, I hope they don't make me fill those hours reading news—what a miserable shift."

Little did I know how many high-profile male television personalities were maneuvering for the spot. Filling Imus's shoes was a very big deal.

A few days after the Imus firing, I bumped into Joe Scarborough, an MSNBC prime-time talk show host and former Florida congressman. Joe worked out of a studio in Pensacola, Florida, and he was in town to audition for the Imus slot. I had never met him, and knew his face only because when I read my news cut-ins in the network control room every evening, I would do what's called a toss back to his news and opinion show, *Scarborough Country*, and his face would pop up on the monitors in front of me. Every night at 7:59, I'd say, "That's a look at the news. Now back to *Scarborough Country*." I never watched the show because I was always yanking off my microphone and hurrying back to find new ways to fill my downtime.

Joe introduced himself, and after a brief conversation I could see wheels turning in his head. He asked me if I would be interested in hosting the morning show with him. My answer was, "Why?" His question didn't make any sense. I told him I was a forty-year-old washed-up newswoman and housewife from Westchester. His response was, "Exactly! Someone real!" He was dead serious. I was thrown off, because I was serious, too: I knew what television executives were looking for, and it wasn't me. But Joe seemed to recognize the contribution I could make to the show. I liked that. He seemed to want me *as myself,* rather than someone acting the part of a television cohost. If he meant what he said, it would be an intriguing opportunity.

Still, I was reticent about signing on to an early morning show that would throw my household into disarray. My family had put up with my crazy nights and early-morning shifts many times as I was scrambling up the career ladder, and they had picked me up after it collapsed beneath me. Why would I put them through that again? Why would I want to put myself through it again? Did I need a demanding job in television, or did I need a predictable one? After all I'd been through, I realized I was kind of happy with the predictable, and I was reluctant to put everything on the line again.

But Joe is nothing if not persuasive. He was hyperfocused on his concept for a groundbreaking political talk show. There would be no rehearsal and no script, just a cast of sharp journalists and analysts, all handpicked by him, who could engage in lively and intelligent discussions while treating one another with respect. He wanted real conversation, long interviews, true reactions. He was determined to make his vision of the show a reality. He knew what he wanted, and what he wanted was for me to be his cohost.

My gut told me that he was gifted. That he had a really good idea, and that his idea was going to change the way news was delivered on television. Joe's concepts seemed exciting and innovative to me as a woman who had spent two decades in an industry that did little more than rehash tired news formats. This show would be a wild ride, and Joe was inviting me along.

I didn't really know what I was stepping into on that first day back in 2007. But within seconds of being on the air together, I knew I was a part of something unique. That morning, I was on the set at 5:55 AM. Joe and I began discussing the latest political news before the cameras started rolling, and we just kept talking as the program went live. "Five, four, three, two, one . . ." We just kept talking. In a random trick of fate, we had immediate on-air chemistry. We had only met the day before, but you would have thought we had been at this for years.

I have been on my share of new shows; you can tell very quickly if something works or not. Most are duds. I knew immediately *Morning Joe* would be a hit. Much of TV is conventional and safe; each show gets tied up with a neat little bow at the end. But this show was different. It was unpredictable and risky, and extremely smart. Both Joe and I had been beaten up in our respective careers, and that experience—plus the fact that we were both bored by the traditional television news format—made us fearless. I thought to myself, "This is the kind of breakthrough show I'd want my girls to see me host. I like watching this, and I like doing this."

When we heard we'd won the Imus slot, we were off and running.

From that moment, our team began working around the clock to build *Morning Joe* into the success it is today. We had a tiny staff and limited resources, but we had big plans and even more determination. We didn't engage in shrill dialogue to win ratings or deliver packaged reports that were safe and pat. We told the truth as we saw it. We said what we thought, and sometimes we were wrong. We were ourselves, come what may, and people responded immediately. Everyone knew that we all cared to be there despite our differences, and we all genuinely liked one another.

Ours would become the show that the *New York Times* described as "unlike anything else on morning television," that the *New Yorker* called "appallingly entertaining," and that *Forbes* magazine proclaimed "the hottest morning show around." But it would take a Herculean effort to get there.

Joe was the creator. I was the executor. He focused on ideas and pushed them through the MSNBC hierarchy. He fought for my job, our producer Chris Licht's job, and other on- and off-air people whom he felt were the right fit. Building the team took up most of his day after we got off the air. He brought on Willie Geist as the bright young personality who would add youth and attitude. My job was to bring in the big-name newsmakers to our brand-new, and at that point unknown, very early morning show. I took my Black-Berry everywhere and worked it around the clock.

I used all the skills I had developed from years of chasing stories as a reporter. I worked every angle, every connection. I got up at three AM every day, but if I needed to call a contact at eight PM, I pushed myself to sound perky and awake. Aggressive. On a mission. I kept the phone at my ear while I jogged. As Joe and Chris and I would have strategy sessions, I would thump along my four-mile route, panting, sweating, and thinking, "How can we make the show better?"

18

The three of us realized we had stumbled onto a rare opportunity in the odd and unpredictable world of TV news and "opinion television." We had been given a three-hour window over which we had complete control. MSNBC was still busy dealing with the fallout of the Imus situation, and as with many new shows, the network simply let ours fly to see how it did on its own.

I have to hand it to MSNBC president Phil Griffin. He knew we were on to something and that we needed space to work out the kinks. Only a confident, sharp manager would have had that foresight. There are not many of his kind in television news. He fought for us and protected us from unnecessary tweaking from upstairs.

Before long, *Morning Joe*'s future was looking bright, but mine still wasn't. The network brass weren't convinced that I was the right cohost. They gave me a new contract and moved me from freelance into a staff position, but the money was barely better, and I was not formally assigned to *Morning Joe*. That meant I had to be available to work for any and every other show that needed me. My days began with a four AM commute into New Jersey, where I would trudge up to the makeup room and have my face painted; most days I didn't scrape that makeup off for sixteen hours. Often I would be on the air four or five hours a day, then spend the rest of my waking hours chasing guests for the next day's *Morning Joe* and doing any other jobs that MSNBC assigned. I didn't want to seem difficult by turning down extra assignments. I figured if management was asking me to take on more, that meant they had actually considered my workload and felt I should be able to handle additional tasks.

The ink on my new contract was barely dry when I realized my mistake.

Joe and I worked so closely as we put this show together that we pretty much knew everything about each other. He'd answer my phone and talk to my kids, and I'd answer his phone and talk to his. Phil called, or Joe's agent called, and they'd negotiate a detail in his latest contract, and I'd be sitting right there listening. So I knew there was a vast difference in our salaries. We talked openly about the money he was getting and the money that I should be getting. He was very concerned and hoped that I would be a permanent part of the show, and I think we were both just relieved when I finally had a contract in hand.

The reality of my situation began to dawn on me when I learned that Willie Geist had just re-signed as well, but his was a contract to be on the show, whereas mine was simply to be on MSNBC. Someone had said, "Just sign this," and I signed a generic contract that had me working on any shift, including *Morning Joe*, but without the title "*Morning Joe* cohost." It said MSNBC could also ask me to do *Nightly News* pieces, *Weekend Today* news reading, and hours and hours filling in for other anchors in the afternoon. Willie was smarter about the negotiation and cut himself a better deal. He asked for what he wanted, and he didn't show up at work until he got it. When I heard through the grapevine that he was making more than I was, I realized I had done myself a great disservice. I didn't value myself, and I had taken a deal that reflected that.

I was stunned to learn that Willie made more, but I was happy for him. I've always known he's a great talent, and I'm sure his value will explode in coming years. I'm good at predicting these things for other people. I just couldn't believe how stupid I'd been on my own behalf, how my own sense of value was so deflated by low self-esteem and a misplaced sense of gratitude. I was demoralized, but I was determined to show up shining every morning. Balancing the job, the family, and the hours was exhausting, but knowing that what appeared to be a career high was really a complete failure was truly depressing.

Living with that reality was bringing out an emotion in me that does not work for a woman in the workplace, at least not mine: anger. *Morning Joe* shows me at my best and my worst. Our show is transparent and real. We hide nothing. It all shows: the effects of exhaustion (and Ambien), all our moods and emotions. I knew anger wouldn't rate. I would have to find a way to be happy, or at least at peace.

I had taken a tremendous risk in accepting this job. I didn't have financial security, and my career was hanging in the balance. On top of that, I was working with a man who refused to follow a conventional path. Some called him a rule breaker. But I knew he was actually a game changer.

That same rebellious streak that ruffled feathers in Congress made Joe a controversial figure in the halls of NBC. While everybody else played it safe, Joe demanded that we push the envelope. Needless to say, that earned me few new friends at 30 Rock. Many tried to talk me out of working with him, even offering me the "safety" of a slot on another "more legitimate" broadcast. But I refused to listen to them. I went in a different direction, and I'm extremely proud of that fact. I don't know any women who would have done what I did in that instance. I went my own way, ripped up my own script. That takes experience and self-knowledge. The ability to be brave, to try something new, to take a risk, to know it's good when it's good—that's worth something. And if you're going to take a major risk, you sure as hell better know what it's worth. I can do that. I'm proud because accepting the co-host job meant accepting so much risk. And so much fighting. And so much standing up in the face of rejection. Of so much push back from NBC management and my new bosses who I instinctively wanted to please.

But I was still clueless when it came to translating that powerful sense of self-worth into actual dollars and cents.

Despite the money, I didn't think of leaving. I was invested in *Morning Joe* and engrossed in the story we were covering: the 2008 race for the White House. The combination of the first African-American major-party nominee and the lightning speed of the news cycle in the age of social media made the 2008 presidential race unlike any other election I had covered.

Instead of walking away from MSNBC when I first realized I was underpaid, I worked harder to get the candidates booked on our show. It helped that my brother Ian worked for McCain; my father, former national security adviser to

President Carter, had endorsed Obama early on; and my other brother, Mark, worked for President Clinton and was joining the Obama organization to help out. If I didn't know someone at a campaign, I'd bluff my way in until I got to know someone. Before long, I had lined up interviews with every candidate from Barack Obama to Ron Paul.

Joe and I knew that this election was our opportunity to really put *Morning Joe* on the map. No one was going to do it for us. We would do everything for ourselves.

Other morning shows had a staff of forty to fifty people and the full support of being "management's choice"; we had a staff of eight, our BlackBerrys, and the belief that we could do it. We knew we had to be scrappy and relentless. So we ran around the country, basically carrying the show on our backs, and working around the clock to make it must-see political TV.

There was no better example of how alone we were at times than the Iowa caucuses. We wanted to take *Morning Joe* to Iowa, but MSNBC wasn't sold on it enough at that point to spend the money. Management liked us, just not that much. We knew we had to be on the ground in Iowa. We fought and fought, and still hit brick walls. They told us there was not enough room in the budget and not enough room in the convention center, where all the other networks had built their sets.

Joe, Chris, and I refused to take no for an answer. We forged ahead. I kept calling all the campaigns and asking them to stop by our studio set—a set that did not yet exist in the minds of MSNBC management. Chris worked on the travel and producing details as if we were going. On the eve of New Year's weekend, Joe called Phil Griffin and laid down the law. "Phil, we are going to Iowa," he said. "If you want us on the air on Monday, you might want to send a few cameras. If you don't, you will have shots of empty chairs in New York. Your call, but *we are going to Iowa.*"

MSNBC finally gave Phil the money, and within 48 hours we were scrambling to kiss our families good-bye and make our flights. Joe flew from Florida and made it there first. But Chris and I got stuck in Chicago because of storms and air-traffic delays. We had ten hours to make it to Des Moines, 300 miles away. Chris and I grabbed a rental car—without my luggage, because it was lost. We drove all night through a blizzard to make our five-AM Des Moines broadcast. We arrived several hours before airtime. I was so worn down, I even ate McDonald's chicken nuggets and fries for breakfast; as someone who aspires to be a paragon of healthy living, that was a desperate act.

With no room for a *Morning Joe* set at the convention center, we set up a makeshift studio at Java Joe's, a popular Des Moines coffee shop filled with locals. Soon, every candidate showed up at Java Joe's and stayed a while to drink coffee and shoot the breeze. The result was spontaneous and spirited conversations that engrossed viewers and participants alike.

I was running on no sleep but made it through five hours of programming that morning. After seeing the first hour of the show—the show no one wanted to send to Iowa—Phil got so excited that he asked us to stay on the air two extra hours.

24

MSNBC's front office would later tell us those five hours were among the network's best hours of campaign coverage.

It was at Java Joe's that we received the blessing from the king of political news, *NBC News'* Washington bureau chief and moderator of *Meet the Press*, Tim Russert. He was over at the convention center doing the *Today Show*, but it was clear to Tim that the excitement in Iowa was at Java Joe's. When the door swung open and Tim walked in saying, "Hey, you guys mind if I get on the show?" we were thrilled. He stayed on for an hour and then hung out in the background for the rest of the morning talking to candidates and campaign managers. The whole morning flew by and felt like magic.

Phil Griffin had already given us some unforgettable advice: "You all should look at it this way: You have an audience of one. You need to ask yourself, 'Would Tim like this?'" So when Tim, the head of the network's political coverage, joined us at the center of the action, it was as if we'd received a true royal blessing. We believe Tim's support and presence helped set the path for our future. He passed away in June of 2008, but we will never forget what he did for us. We will never forget our audience of one.

Phil called Joe during the broadcast the second day. "Hey, can you do this in New Hampshire too?" he asked. "And what about Michigan and South Carolina?"

All our hard work was paying off. Our ratings soared. MSNBC was keeping us on the air an extra three hours every day, six in total. *Morning Joe* had quickly become *the* place for presidential candidates to be seen and heard. It was the show of choice for political junkies and viewers tired of the standard morning broadcast fare. Our audience was growing, and the show itself was making news.

While we were on the road, I tried to push my salary concerns aside. I didn't want to deal with the situation; I certainly didn't have time. Yet the money issue kept surfacing. At times when I should have been celebrating, I grew morose and discouraged.

PLAYING THE VICTIM

Three months into *Morning Joe's* run, I started getting e-mails making fun of my clothes. One day I wore a vivid pattern, and a viewer wrote, "What painter threw up on Mika?"

Part of my job is to look fresh sitting among a bunch of men at six AM. In a visual medium, appearances matter. Clothes are part of the production element of a talk show. If not handled correctly, they become a distraction that interferes with the substance of the broadcast.

That said, nobody cares what the men wear or how they style their hair. Joe rolls out of bed at 5:45 AM and jumps in the car to make the top of the show with only seconds to spare, his face still puffy and creased from sleep. He'll take his seat wearing a fleece sweater and run his hand through his hair to brush it. If he were a woman, he would be called a disgrace.

Being a forty-something woman on TV requires that I wake up around 3:30 every morning and go through a numbing routine in order to look presentable on high-definition TV. A female anchor's hair, makeup, and clothes are scrutinized both inside and outside the network, and if something seems off, she will hear about it in e-mails or even a phone call from the front office.

NBC wasn't providing a wardrobe, so I had to fend for myself on *Morning Joe*. I found out very quickly that it was extremely difficult for me to handle the clothing aspect of being on the air three hours a day. I didn't need Chanel or Gucci, but I needed to look put together and at the very least make sure my clothes and hair were not a distraction. But looking camera-ready requires a wardrobe, and assembling a wardrobe takes a lot of time and costs a lot of money—the two things in my life that were in short supply.

I remember one time running down to the Lord & Taylor near my home and grabbing a bunch of cheap V-neck sweaters. I figured I would save time searching for "new" outfits by simply wearing different colors.

A few weeks later, those sweaters wore out their welcome. I began receiving rude comments via e-mail about wearing the same thing every day. Some of these messages came from determined viewers who managed to find their way into my inbox. If a handful of viewers felt so strongly that they'd try that hard to get through to me, they probably weren't alone.

Clothes and hair were becoming my daily enemy. They represented everything that was wrong with my position at MSNBC. Not only was I was not getting paid what I was worth, but after the added cost of a new wardrobe and quality haircuts I was actually losing money by working at the network.

I knew I deserved a raise. I knew I needed a raise. But I still felt anxious about asking to be compensated for what I was bringing to the show. Lots of people considered me a hit, but how did I really know that management agreed? My current salary implied that they still thought of me as a freelancer.

I brought all these feelings with me when I asked for a raise. I actually thought that if I explained to NBC's front office about the clothes and the travel, and how the math didn't make sense, they would respond to my concerns. Looking back (and knowing what I've learned while writing this book), I may as well have said, "Hi. Please don't give me a raise, okay?"

I went to see Phil Griffin, the president of MSNBC, who to this day is a friend, but we didn't know each other that well then. I sat down in his office and said, "I'm sorry if this is bad timing. I don't want to be a problem. I'm absolutely certain that this is a great show. I'm buying clothes for the shift, I'm buying makeup, I'm trying to keep my hair the way it should look." I went on to say, "I really don't want to be a diva or high maintenance or anything. But the way the numbers add up at the end of the month, I need to make more. I really hope you can understand that."

I was nervous and struggling to articulate both facts and emotions. I was appealing to what I thought would be his . . . what, generous side? It certainly wasn't Phil's job to care about wardrobe details, and I had signed an agreement. The conversation was a disaster. Needless to say I left Phil's office without a raise, but it would be unfair to focus the blame on him. At that time I still didn't realize why my plea failed. I didn't know what was wrong with my approach, and given my age and professional experience, that's simply not right.

By the time we returned to New York from covering the primaries, the tension was building. We were still working like hell, moving on to Election Day and the inauguration. It was a constant, driving battle. Every day I could feel myself edging one step closer to the breaking point. I was doing four long hours, and the guys were lumbering off the set at nine, going to relax in their offices. I'd continue to book the show, and push the show, and travel for the show into the night. Every day I grew tenser and tenser; again, it was nobody's fault but my own.

I knew there was really no point in blaming Joe or Willie. I liked them, and they deserved everything they were getting and more. They were smart enough to get it. That was clear with every meeting that we had with management and every phone call that I overheard. The men around me were doing a good job of getting what they wanted and deserved. The inequity became tougher to overlook.

I was angry at myself, and certainly my family was paying the price at home all over again. I'd gone from unemployed to finding a freelance job that was totally doable and a good transition for them, to quite frankly working harder than I ever did at *60 Minutes*, which really seemed like the ultimate in exhausting, hard-driving, competitive, tough, constantly explosive, stressful work. But this was even more intense and all-consuming.

Joe was growing more furious by the day. He had believed in me from the start, and he wanted me to focus solely on *Morning Joe*. He probably saw me getting in my own way as I tried to get my due, but being aware of the challenges all women in television face, he knew how difficult it would be for me to solve this problem on my own. It never occurred to me during this time that it was my job to just say no. Many days I was exhausted and depressed. I would tell myself if I worked harder, I'd prove my worth and eventually the bosses would notice and reward me.

It would be a fruitless wait on my part.

CHAPTER 2

GET OUT OF YOUR WAY
Women as Their Own Worst Enemies

MY STORY, WITH VALERIE JARRETT, TINA BROWN, CAROL SMITH, SHERYL SANDBERG, CAROL BARTZ, LESLEY JANE SEYMOUR, NORA EPHRON, ARIANNA HUFFINGTON, AND SUZE ORMAN

THE PARIS HILTON INCIDENT

Despite the network's misgivings, Joe and I knew that our partnership on the air was driving the show's appeal. In fact, just one month into our run, our chemistry would put *Morning Joe* on the map.

The show's fans know it as "the Paris Hilton incident." The story began the morning socialite Paris Hilton, released from prison after serving minimal time for violating probation, walked through a blinding gauntlet of frenzied photographers. Her release was written as the lead for our news-headlines segment on a day when the Iraq war should have been at the head. I couldn't believe this junk was being passed off as news, so Joe and I called it out by mocking ourselves and the news business as a whole. At first I held up the news script and simply announced I wouldn't read it; then Joe goaded me into ripping, burning, and shredding it at the top of each hour of our three-hour show.

The episode was emblematic of what makes the *Morning Joe* chemistry work: our ability to act instinctively and say what we think without fear. We call each other out. We call other journalists out. We call politicians out. We do it with humor and transparency, and we do it with the credibility of having been there: we're guided by our collective experience in the fields of politics and news. Our life lessons have taught us many things, including not to take ourselves too seriously.

Ripping up the script was an unremarkable act to the *Morning Joe* team, but we discovered that in the world of 24/7 news, it was a minor league sensation. For some reason, the Paris Hilton incident hit a nerve. Someone posted the video clip on YouTube and it went viral, seen by millions of viewers around the world. The incident helped introduce *Morning Joe* to a whole new set of viewers. To this day, I am applauded and thanked by rabid news junkies who say they will never forget that moment. They tell us repeatedly that our show is refreshing because all the players are candid about their beliefs and biases, which apparently is something viewers have been looking for.

Was my value suddenly changing? Could it be that what looked like "forty and washed-up" was now "experienced and gutsy"? Joe had assured me of that every step of the way. But I was programmed differently. I had my doubts.

The day after the Paris Hilton incident, a top NBC executive, a woman, called me into her office and asked me to take a seat. Her stern expression told me that this was not a victory lap. She was clearly unhappy that I had ripped up the Paris Hilton script. In a sharp tone she warned me that I would now have a reputation for being a "problem" and "difficult." She was "concerned" that people "wouldn't like" me.

What did I do? I *apologized.*

As she paced her office looking like she was about to fire me, her assistant barged in with an urgent call. She left the room. I sat there alone, wondering whether I had apologized enough.

Five minutes later, the executive returned. I don't know who had been on the other end of that urgent call or what was said, but her tone and body language had done a sudden 180. "We want to offer you your own show," she said brightly, "at nine AM, after *Morning Joe.* A full hour. All yours. You get to cohost *Morning Joe*, and then you get to host your own show. All yours!"

I must have had a slight case of whiplash. Clearly I wasn't thinking straight, because what did I do next?

I *thanked* her.

Seriously.

My success on *Morning Joe* meant that I would now be responsible for another hour of television every day. While it may look casual and spontaneous, hosting *Morning Joe*, a political show with no teleprompter or safety net, is incredibly demanding work. Its success depends on my instincts, my up-to-the-minute knowledge of world events and my mind being clear so that I can ad-lib no matter the situation. Three hours of extemporaneous discussion and debate were considered a hard slog for any television host or anchor.

As I looked around the table on the *Morning Joe* set the next day, I realized what I had done. Joe and Willie stretched and yawned at the end of our three hours and talked about how tired they were and how our schedule was insane. Then they wandered off the set to finally collapse somewhere. I was just getting started on an additional full hour, an hour I would now have to fill every day. By myself. I was still the lowest-paid on the set despite four hours each day on the air. No other anchor on television worked those hours five days a week. At the end of every *Morning Joe*, at 8:55 Eastern Time, we have a short segment where we all take a turn saying what we've learned that day. That morning I should have said "I learned that I am an ass." How could I have missed this opportunity to ask for what I deserved?

But as I started talking to women, especially researchers, I heard many stories and statistics that surprised me. The simple fact is that women don't ask for raises as often as men do. My problem wasn't just a personal failing, it was a common experience.

* * *

According to our MSNBC online survey, men are more likely than women to ask for raises or promotions, and men ask for more raises or pro-

motions over the course of their careers than women do.

* * *

More than a quarter of women in our survey described themselves as scared when asking for a raise. Many said they would rather have a root canal.

* * *

Men were more likely to say they feel confident and up for the challenge.

* * *

In the first of many conversations with successful women, I sat down with Obama senior adviser Valerie Jarrett and shared my story. She listened and nodded all too knowingly.

"We are our own worst enemy," Jarrett says, understanding exactly how I had been tripped up. "Somehow it's unseemly for women to promote themselves. We think that there's a meritocracy that's hierarchical, and the people at the top make the decisions about what promotions are based on."

As a female and an African-American, Jarrett says she always expected to face obstacles in the workplace: "My parents raised me to think because I was a girl and because I was black I was going to have to work twice as hard. They did it with no chip on their shoulder—it was just a fact of life, get used to it. Don't try to change what is, just work twice as hard."

So she says that's what she did. She worked hard and kept her head down. But Jarrett didn't expect that working hard would not automatically lead to advancement and better pay.

* * *

"I felt like if I was deserving, then my boss should recognize that I was deserving."—VALERIE JARRETT

* * *

"I kept doing more and more work," Jarrett tells me. She describes an experience she had when she worked in the real estate division of the City of Chicago's Department of Law early in her career. Jarrett felt fortunate to have the job, but she wasn't advancing. She says she was lucky to have a female mentor, Lucille Dobbins, who instructed her: "Lucille said to me, 'You are doing more work than your supervisor and your supervisor's supervisor . . . you should be a deputy.' I said, 'Well my boss knows I'm working hard, and he values what I'm doing.' She said, 'You can't sit around waiting for people to recognize your work, you have to ask for it. You need to go in there and tell him you should be a deputy. And you should tell him you want to be in the front suite of offices, because he doesn't have a woman in the front suite.'"

"Did that seem weird to you?" I ask.

"It seemed like absolutely horrible advice," Jarrett answers. "I thought [my boss] would humiliate me and tell me to get out of his office."

Still, Jarrett gathered her courage and went for it. "I said, 'This is the work I'm doing, this is the level of complexity, and I really think I should be a deputy,'" she tells me. "He looked at me and said, 'Okay.'"

Jarrett was shocked. She got the promotion and the front office. "I felt that if I was deserving, then my boss should recognize that I was deserving," she reasons. "That's what bosses do."

Jarrett says her mentor taught her an important lesson: "What Lucille brought to my attention was that I was not valuing my own work and that I needed to be my own best advocate. And that is something that women seldom do and men do intuitively. Men ask for it all the time. Women never do. Women expect that if you do really well, someone will recognize your performance and will reward you accordingly."

While this seems obvious, for many women—even a top presidential adviser—simply asking can be difficult. Jarrett says that asking for that promotion "was one of the most uncomfortable conversations that I have ever had."

* * *

"If you're not asking for a promotion . . . you're not going to get the gold ring."—VALERIE JARRETT

* * *

Jarrett says that while we women sit around waiting, men are busy charging the hill. "If you're number four, five or six, and there's a guy who's four, five or six he's going to ask to be number one," she points out. "If you're not asking for a promotion and you're waiting for your merit to be recognized, men are going to hire you to be close, but you're not going to get the gold ring."

Tina Brown—journalist; author; cofounder of *The Daily Beast*; regular on *Morning Joe*; and the recently-appointed editor-in-chief of *Newsweek*, the first woman to hold the position in the magazine's 78-year history—told me a similar story, but from the perspective of a boss.

Brown is a friend and mentor, and a regular on the show. Our lives are a constant swirl, and in order to get a few moments to talk about the subject of women and compensation, we had to seize the moment. I ended up sitting down with her in a cold dressing room in between segments on *Morning Joe*. She had her coat on, ready to run to the airport and catch a flight, but she took the time to think aloud on this issue and share her valuable perspective.

"I was in a situation recently, within *The Daily Beast*, where I realized I had overlooked a woman who had been doing a fantastic job. We had brought a man in to do the job, and he failed, horribly. And then we hired another person, who came in and failed. Finally the woman came to see someone at the company and said, 'Look, I've sat here, and I've seen two guys fail at this job. What about me?'"

Brown was astonished that she'd overlooked this person once, let alone twice: "I said to my executive editor, 'You know, this is terrible. The first time someone failed, we should have gone to her . . . She's clearly so much better.'" Brown says that she was ashamed she hadn't recognized the female employee's value in the first place. But that said, the employee hadn't stepped up and asked for the work.

Brown wasn't the only female manager who admitted making that same mistake. Women employees just don't seem to have the confidence to raise their hand, to put it out there, to say "Hey! I'm worth this!" So they're overlooked by female bosses and male bosses alike.

* * *

"We women think that we will work very very hard . . . and then money will come."
—Carol Smith

* * *

After an extensive career at Time Warner and nearly a decade as the chief brand officer at *Elle*, Carol Smith has employed thousands of women during her years of overseeing women's magazines. She admits she sees women like me all the time: "We women think we will work very, very hard—we will work harder than anybody in the office—we will get the gold star, and then the money will come. When the money doesn't come, instead of walking into the boss's office and saying, 'I've done this, I've done this, I've done this, and now I need this,' we sit around and earn one fifteenth of what the man next door earns.

"I think what we have to do is recognize that if we don't ask, it's not coming our way. Men ask all the time; it's not that [the money] just comes to them. I swear it doesn't," Smith says.

Why don't we ask? That's a good question.

Linda Babcock, a professor of economics at Carnegie Mellon University and researcher on the subject of women and negotiation, cowrote a fascinating book called *Women Don't Ask*. Babcock says women ask for raises and promotions eighty-five percent less often than their male counterparts. And when women do ask, on average they ask for thirty percent less.

One of the reasons women don't ask, she argues, is that they don't realize that opportunities exist. Babcock writes, "One of the major barriers preventing women from asking for what they need more of the time is their perception that their circumstances are more fixed and absolute—less negotiable—than they really are."

* * *

"I just felt lucky to have the opportunity."
—SHERYL SANDBERG

* * *

At the age of forty-one, Sheryl Sandberg has achieved extraordinary success. When she agreed to talk to me for this book, I actually got nervous. Surely her experiences must be very different. What if she debunked all my theories?

Sandberg served as chief of staff for the United States Department of the Treasury before leaving government to become vice president of global online sales and operations at Google. She's now the chief operating officer of the social networking giant Facebook. Sandberg clearly knows her stuff about gender dynamics as well as social media.

When I ask whether she believes my struggle to be fairly compensated is a common problem, she immediately agrees: "The data clearly show men own their success more than women do. Men are more likely to overestimate and women are more likely to underestimate performance on objective criteria. So if you look at something like grade point average and you survey men and women on what their GPAs were, men get it wrong slightly high and women get it wrong slightly low."

So men are more likely to think of themselves as more successful and women are more likely to think of themselves as less successful, even if their achievements are the same. Sandberg also points out that men ascribe their success to their own skills, whereas women ascribe their success to outside sources.

"So if you ask a man, 'Why were you successful?' the man will say, 'You know, because of myself,'" Sandberg says. "And the women will say, 'Because I got lucky and these great people I work with helped me.' So think of the situation in which men are getting it wrong slightly high, and women slightly low. Men think it's them; women don't. So why does that matter? It matters because I think a lot of getting ahead in the workplace has to do with being willing to raise your hand and say I want that job, I'll take on that challenge—or better yet, I see that problem and I'm going to fix it. That comes back to self-confidence. So when men feel more confident they raise their hand; when women feel less confident they take their hand down."

* * *

"A lot of getting ahead in the workplace has to do with being willing to raise your hand."
—SHERYL SANDBERG

* * *

Knowing your value means owning your success. Owning your success means acknowledging your achievements. By acknowledging achievements you build confidence.

Sandberg gives me a striking example from her own experience. She was giving a talk about owning one's success to 150 or so Facebook employees, and she mentioned the GPA experiment. At the end of the talk Sandberg told the audience she had time for two more questions. She answered them, but hands were waving so she continued to call on people.

Afterward she went back to her desk and found a young woman waiting for her. Sandberg asked if she'd learned anything from the talk, and the young woman said, "I learned to keep my hand up." Sandberg asked what she meant, and the woman told her, "After you took those two final questions, I put my hand down and all the other women put their hands down. A bunch of men kept their hands up and then you took more questions."

The men ignored the question limit and went for it, keeping their hands in the air. What did they have to lose? Nothing. Sandberg saw more waving hands and took their questions.

42

Sandberg admits she didn't notice that only women had taken their hands down, because after all, why would she have noticed what wasn't there? She says that proved her point right there: "If we as women don't raise our hands in the workplace, we're not going to get the same opportunities men do. Because men keep their hands up."

Despite her many achievements, Sandberg tells me a story of how she herself failed to raise her hand and how it almost cost her a lot of money.

"I was getting a new position. I got an offer to do the job, and I thought the offer was really great, and I was going to take it," Sandberg says. "My brother-in-law kept saying, 'You gotta negotiate. They want you to take on all this responsibility—ask for more compensation.' My response was, 'This is such a great opportunity. I'm so lucky to get it, and it's such a generous offer, I'm not going to negotiate.'" But Sandberg says her brother-in-law kept pushing: "He said, 'Goddamn it, Sheryl, why are you agreeing to make half of what any man would make to do this?'"

Finally, that motivated her. Sandberg says that after her brother-in-law convinced her to ask for more, "I went in and asked, and they moved up considerably. Had I not asked, they wouldn't have. But the reason I wouldn't have asked is because I just felt lucky to have the opportunity." Her story sounded all too familiar to me. I've always been in awe of Sandberg, and the idea that she and I shared a common failing was cracking the superhero image I had of her. I appreciate her honesty. And I realize now that women must get over feeling lucky. The time has come to turn the page.

Sandberg sent my daughters and me some Facebook T-shirts. I wear mine feeling a kinship with this powerful woman, who didn't know her "face" value, even as she reached the top of the ladder.

* * *

"I was just happy to have the professional position."—Carol Bartz

* * *

My experience with the CEO of Yahoo, Carol Bartz, was also an eye-opener. To borrow the famous line from the movie *When Harry Met Sally*, "I'll have what she's having!"

Bartz is a rarity in today's corporate world: she's among the select women heading three percent of Fortune 500 companies and one of only a handful heading a technology firm. When I ask her whether she has ever had trouble getting paid what she's worth, her reply is immediate: "Oh, honest to god, I think every step of the way. There's no question about that."

Bartz tells me that in the early 1990s, she was competing with two men to be CEO of Autodesk, a multinational design software company. She got the job and ended up with what she thought was a generous compensation package. But she later found out that the men she was up against had been asking for millions more. Says Bartz: "What they were negotiating for was way over—*way* over what they had negotiated with me . . . you know, I was too naïve, too stupid, and they got me on the cheap . . . when I found out what the guys were asking, I thought, 'You dummy.'"

Bartz says that early on in her career, she had difficulty promoting herself. "When I was younger, I was just happy to have the professional position," she tells me. "Then I think you naïvely put your head in the sand, and think they will notice your worth."

I was struck by the fact that both Bartz and Sandberg were telling me stories about not knowing their value, and feeling lucky to get the offers they did. I had assumed their psychology would be different, and that they had handled themselves very differently. Hearing these women talk about luck struck a chord with me. My feeling lucky to have a job had cost me dearly over the years. Feeling lucky and fearing rejection. Women who run women's magazines are extremely in tune with those sentiments that drive us or get in our way. On this issue, they let it rip.

Lesley Jane Seymour, the editor-in-chief of *More* magazine, the leading lifestyle magazine for women of substance and style, is a great promoter of women. She is a wife and mom, and she is also a friend and mentor.

She tells me, "If you talk to a lot of women as you're doing this, you're going to hear a lot of women use the word *luck*. I hear executives all the time say, 'I'm lucky to have gotten here, I'm lucky' . . . I can't even tell you how many successful females, CEOs of companies, will say 'I just got lucky.' But if you think it's just luck that made you successful, then if you ask for too much, the luck might just run out."

"Emotion can trip women up," Seymour says when she hears my story. "We are willing to take those substitutes because we have been brought up on emotion." Seymour, who has run several magazines in the thirty-some years she's been in publishing, said it took her years to realize that feeling "loved" by her bosses did not mean she was being valued. "I definitely made the mistake in my career of looking for an emotional connection instead of just money. I used to tell my boss that I would do the job 'even if you didn't pay me,'" Seymour says, laughing. "I guess they decided to take me at my word." She would later discover that colleagues with the same responsibilities had larger salaries.

* * *

"We are willing to take those substitutes because we have been brought up on emotion."
—LESLEY JANE SEYMOUR

* * *

"I ran each magazine basically with the idea I was going to run it as if it were my own product, my own business, with my own money . . . I'm going to make the best choices because I'm running it as if it's mine, I'm putting in 120 hours a week, and I'm saving them money, they're going to love me so much . . . And guess what. They didn't care!"

Seymour says her bosses quickly figured out that she'd accept approval instead of money. "I had one boss who was very good. For instance, once when I had a really good year, she took me out to lunch and she gave me a pair of earrings. Jeweled earrings. She told me how much the company loved me. That was very smart. That's something that women are susceptible to. No man is going to take another man out to lunch, give him a pair of earrings and say how much the company loves him. The guy would say 'What's wrong with this company?' I mean, my husband would laugh hysterically and walk out. His response would be, 'What kind of company is this? Give me a raise!' Instead, my first reaction was, 'Oh my god, thank you, you love me so much!'"

Bottom line, says Seymour: "The men's way of doing business is without emotion. It's just money. It's just business. Emotions play absolutely no hand in business in America in general. You have to bring as little emotion as you can to it."

* * *

"You can't expect men to take us seriously if we don't take ourselves seriously. That is just the truth. It would be sweet if they did."
—NORA EPHRON

* * *

Movie director, producer, screenwriter, author, and playwright Nora Ephron tells me, "I think several things are more true about women than they are about men in terms of knowing your value. One is that women have a constitutional resistance to quitting. We like to be good. We like to be loyal. We like to be good girls. One of the ways you make more money in the work place is by quitting and going someplace else. It's always been my feeling that women just don't get that, they don't learn that lesson that men constantly teach, which is you have to keep moving in order to get raises."

47

Ephron says this was true of her early career, when she was working at *Esquire* magazine. She was thrilled to be working there, even though she was being paid something like a thousand dollars per month. "I was married at the time, and I didn't have to make a lot of money because there were two incomes," she says. "Then my marriage broke up, and the editor of *New York Magazine* called and offered me three times as much as I was making at *Esquire*. First of all I needed the money, but second of all I was so stunned by it. I went to the editor of *Esquire* and I said, 'I've had this offer from *New York Magazine*.' And he said, 'We'll match it.' Then I got really irritated, because I thought, 'Why did I have to ask for this?' And then after I got done thinking that, I thought, 'Well it's my fault—I should have asked for it!'"

In hindsight, Ephron says she just wasn't taking herself as seriously as she should have. She didn't know her value, and to some degree she didn't care, because she was so happy to be working at that particular magazine. Ultimately she went to *New York Magazine* simply because she was so annoyed that she'd been underpaid and had worked for so long without realizing it.

Ephron doesn't blame women, but tells me the problem is that "We don't take ourselves seriously. We can't expect men to take us seriously if we don't take ourselves seriously. That is just the truth. It would be sweet if they did and we didn't have to do anything. But that's what we want; we don't want to have to do anything. We don't want people thinking that we're pushy or masculine."

Arianna Huffington—high-profile columnist, author, and

cofounder and editor-in-chief of *The Huffington Post*—has been a friend and a supporter of mine since *Morning Joe* began. She agrees that asking for a raise is an area fraught with anxiety for many women. "One reason is that most women have a very different relationship to money than men do," she tells me. "For us, money represents love, power, security, control, self-worth, independence. After all, if money were just money, everyone would always make rational decisions about it. And we know women certainly don't always do that. But why? One reason is that women have been raised to think of money in terms of security—and not just financial security. Even today, a surprising number of us still think that it's the man's job to make and understand money. Far too often we delegate this responsibility and don't learn enough about money—so of course we fear it."

* * *

"Women don't say what they think, and they don't do what they feel."—SUZE ORMAN

* * *

After she hears my story, financial guru, talk-show host, author, and motivational speaker Suze Orman puts it suc-cinctly: "The problem is, a woman is socialized to accept that which she is given. So if somebody tells you that you can't, you believe it. If somebody says you're not worth it, you be-lieve it. You get angry, but you can't say anything because women don't say what they think and they don't do what they feel."

Wanting to be liked, taking things personally, feeling lucky to have the job, fearing unknown consequences: these are filters through which a lot of women view their work, and that influences the way they react. But the truth is, the filters blur our focus and keep us from our goals.

Looking back at the Paris Hilton incident and the events that followed, I realize it is just one of many cautionary tales I have to share. I would like my story to speak to any and all younger or newly employed women who feel they are "just lucky to be there." Get over being so grateful for the opportunity. If you're good, you should know it and own it, and always be ready to walk. Always be aware of your ability to walk. Depend on no one to notice your worth. Being liked should not be your first priority. I am one hundred percent sure, looking back now, that had I reacted differently when I received my admonition/promotion, my fate would have been different, too. That manager probably would have had more respect for me if I hadn't apologized for ripping up the script. I should have said that I respectfully disagreed with her assessment of the incident, and I should have seized the opportunity to ask for more money. Instead, I did what was asked of me.

CHAPTER 3

WHAT'S A WOMAN WORTH?
The Gender Wage Gap and the Perception of Value

WITH MARIE C. WILSON, ILENE H. LANG, BRIAN NOSEK, TINA BROWN, JACK WELCH, DONALD TRUMP, DONNY DEUTSCH, SUSIE ESSMAN, SENATOR CLAIRE MCCASKILL, BROOKSLEY BORN, SHEILA BAIR, AND HANNAH RILEY BOWLES

NOT YET EQUAL

One could easily argue that women have made impressive gains over the past fifty years. Yes, women now make up more than half the workforce. Yes, we are governors of states and running for president. Yes, there are three women on the Supreme Court, women are commanding space shuttles and serving on Navy submarines. Women in the United States are better educated than men: they receive three college degrees for every two that men earn, they earn more master's degrees than men do, and about forty-three percent of all MBAs. But despite all these impressive gains, we still sell ourselves way too short. On average, women make only seventy-seven cents for every dollar earned by a man. According to a Government Accountability Office study released in September 2010, professional women still make only eighty-one cents for every dollar a man makes in a similar job.

Women are not just lagging in wages; they are far behind when it comes to leadership. Women make up only seventeen percent of the United States Congress. The United States ranks seventy-second of 189 countries in terms of the proportion of women in their national legislatures—behind France and even Afghanistan and Pakistan. Across such industries as business, law, academia, journalism, and politics, on average, women hold fewer than twenty percent of the top positions. Only three percent of Fortune 500 companies have female CEOs. Researchers say that the percentage of women in the executive suites has been growing for decades, but in the past five years that growth has stalled.

So if women are now fifty percent of the workforce, why aren't more women in charge?

PROBLEM? WHAT PROBLEM?

The truth is that the general populace thinks women are already leading across all sectors of the economy. "That's what Deborah Rhode, a scholar at Stanford, wrote of this phenomenon about a decade ago, and it's still true," says women's advocate Marie C. Wilson.

Wilson is a co-creator of Take Our Daughters and Sons to Work Day® and founder and president of the White House Project, a national nonpartisan nonprofit that aims to advance women's leadership in all communities and sectors. The problem, she explained, is that if people think women have already reached parity, the political will doesn't exist to continue fighting for change. "Even though the majority of Americans are comfortable with women leading in all sectors, women's leadership numbers are static at an average of eighteen percent across all ten examined sectors," Wilson says. "When we have actually gotten small groups of CEOs together and interviewed them about why there are not more women leading, they will say, 'I'm not comfortable—I'm just not comfortable.' Some of that is because there are so few women, they think they're going to say the wrong thing." She suggests that men may be hesitant to give women direct feedback for fear of retaliatory lawsuits. And there just aren't enough women leading to fundamentally change the dynamic.

Wilson says that "the magic number seems to be thirty-three percent. If you have one-third women, like you now have on the Supreme Court, it starts to not be about gender, it starts to be about what each of us is talking about. Until you have one-third you are still looked at through a gender lens."

None of this comes as a surprise to women themselves. As columnist Lisa Belkin noted in a recent *New York Times Magazine* article, "Telling women they have reached parity is like telling an unemployed worker the recession is over. It isn't true until it *feels* true." Most women can tell you from personal experience that they've been paid less than men for the same work.

Researchers agree that a lot of the gender wage gap is explainable. Women take time off to have children, so their careers are interrupted and they're not putting in the same number of hours. Women are the caregivers—they're more likely to be the ones taking care of the kids, their aging parents, and their extended family. They also do the majority of housework even when they're the primary breadwinners. Men will choose higher-paying occupations and women will choose more portable (and lower-paying) occupations that allow them to move with a higher-earning spouse. So conventional wisdom says women don't commit as strongly to the labor market, and as a result, they don't earn as much over the course of a lifetime.

But women's choices don't explain everything. "What you find is that when you pull out all of those factors, you still have about forty percent of the wage gap—9.2 cents—unexplained," says Ariane Hegewisch, a study director at the Institute for Women's Policy Research.

SUBCONSCIOUS BIAS

The sad fact is that both men and women are more likely to consider men to be valuable employees. Researchers referred to one experiment in particular that's been repeated in many different places. Ilene H. Lang, a former tech CEO now at the helm of Catalyst, a leading research organization that studies women in the workforce, summed up the findings this way: "Basically, if you take resumes and strip them of names and all gender information, then take the exact same resumes and put a man's name on some with links to a man, and put a woman's name on others with links to a woman, and send them out, hiring managers say that the women are unqualified and the men are terrific candidates. Men get the promotion or job and the women do not. Once you attach a gender link or a gender label, it gets devalued if it's female. This happens over and over again, and it is not because people are intentionally biased or intentionally sexist, but they do not see potential and leadership in women, particularly nonwhite women."

What was really shocking to me was the fact that women were as likely as men to ascribe leadership qualities to men, and dismiss equally qualified women.

Brian Nosek is the director of Project Implicit, a collaboration of scientists at Harvard, the University of Washington, and the University of Virginia. The project uses an online word association test to gauge subconscious bias. For instance, the test measures how quickly you pair words such as *male* and *career*. (The test is on the Web, and anyone can take it: https://implicit.harvard.edu.) When I took it I found that—even though I was writing this book—I, too, subconsciously associate males with career and females with family.

Nosek says these subconscious beliefs could manifest themselves in a variety of ways. For example, "[a manager] may be less likely to ask a female staff member to take a job that requires travel, whereas the same thought might not occur to a manager with a male staffer." And, Nosek points out, this can happen whether the manager is a man or a woman.

When I ask how this might have an impact on my quest for a raise, Nosek says, "The way in which this implicit stereotype might manifest is just a general feeling of not belonging, an uncertainty that this is something I am, or can do . . . whether it's appropriate to even ask, whereas it may not occur to a man in the same situation to even *think* about whether it's appropriate or not. He might think, 'I've been working here three years—time for a raise, damn it!'"

I ask Catalyst President and CEO Ilene H. Lang why women just aren't seen as leaders. One of the reasons, she says, is that bias is perpetuated by the workplace itself. Her organization has studied how employees are chosen in companies that have leadership-development programs. "Most companies have competency-based models . . . They start out by saying, 'Who's successful in our company? What do those successful leaders in our company look like?'" Lang tells me. The companies then design their program for screening high-potential individuals around those key attributes. But because subconscious bias plays its part, the companies end up institutionalizing a preference for men. "The performance-management system will say 'this is how we spot the up-and-coming talent; these are the things you have to be good at,' and, well, when you look at most of those characteristics what you find is that of the top ten, six or seven reflect characteristics of the current leadership, which is most often male," she says.

Like many of us, Tina Brown sees the institutionalized preference for men in action all the time. "You discover with a sort of incredulity that men don't even picture a woman in a job." She offers a recent example in which she was talking to a television executive about staffing changes at his organization: "I asked, 'Who are you thinking of bringing in to be the overall boss of the situation?' And he looked around the room, and he said, 'Well, I was thinking about maybe somebody like—' and he named a guy who was a complete mid-level player, in my judgment. I was incredulous. I'm thinking, 'Wait a minute. Within this organization that we're discussing, I could think of three brilliant women who could easily do that job. They're not even on the drawing board. He's thinking about going outside to a mid-level man who's had a lot of corporate buzz and he's ignoring the three women in the company who I know for a fact are far superior.'"

BEHIND THE STARTING LINE

What surprised me most was the news that most women, even if they get their well-deserved raise, won't ever close the wage gap. Even if women get promotions and raises at the same rate as men, if in their first job they were placed at a lower position and salary than their male colleagues, the same promotion and compensation increase rates will not close the gap. Ilene H. Lang points to a recent Catalyst study of female and male MBA graduates. "Women are pegged at a lower level and lower salary from the very first job out of their MBA program if they start at entry-level. If they are hired at a mid-career level, women and men fare pretty much the same, and they track the same afterward. But somehow, at that entry level, men are seen as much more promising and much more valuable, just because they're men. More women take a hit, just because they're women." So that's hidden bias in action, and where the gender wage gap begins to grow. Says Lang: "The metaphor I use is, imagine that there's a big race and your daughter or your granddaughter or your sister—whoever it is—is really good at track and field and she's training, and she trains with the best of them. She goes to the start line, and you look up and she's not on the start line. She's 100 feet back. Would you accept this? So that's the challenge: women are starting out behind the start line. And they don't catch up."

BUT AREN'T WOMEN GOOD FOR BUSINESS?

These gender disparities exist despite studies that suggest having more women in the top spots boosts the bottom line. That's why the European telecommunications giant Deutsche Telekom mandates that one-third of its top jobs be filled by women. The company's CEO said in a statement, "Taking on more women in management positions is not about the enforcement of misconstrued egalitarianism; having more women at the top will simply help us operate better."

A study by the University of British Columbia's Sauder School of Business found that female CEOs and female company directors tend to pay less in corporate takeovers, creating less debt and saving their shareholders money. Research shows that when more women are on the board of directors, companies are less likely to pay those outrageous compensations we've heard so much about on the news. That's why Norway put a law on the books requiring that at least forty percent of the boards of directors of public companies be female.

Much of the research about gender and performance, however, is still under debate. Academics who challenge the current findings ask, "If companies that hire more women do better, how do we really know what role women play in that success? Are companies that seek out divergent perspectives simply more innovative and therefore make more money?"

Curiously, two men I interviewed—both of them tremendously successful captains of industry—argued that there's no substantial difference between male and female executives at the very top. Both Jack Welch and Donald Trump argue that the best corporate leaders are gender-neutral.

* * *

"When you get a good woman leader, she is every bit as good as a man . . . good leaders are gender-neutral."—JACK WELCH

* * *

In his twenty years as CEO of General Electric, the parent company of NBC, Jack Welch was credited with turning that company into one of America's largest and most valuable. His management skills are legendary, and earned him a reputation as one of America's toughest bosses. If his managers weren't producing, they no longer had a job.

I present Welch with the theory I'd heard from other interviewees, that executives love hiring women because women work harder and aren't always asking for things like bigger offices and more money, and they don't spend a lot of time drawing attention to themselves and self-promoting. Does he agree?

Welch takes the contrarian point of view: "I think the distinction in many ways is a phony distinction. A players, really great managers and leaders, are almost gender-neutral. When you get a good woman leader, she is every bit as good as a man and has many of the same characteristics. One thing I would say is that certain industries are much more amenable to women leaders and they all will be eventually . . . But good leaders are gender-neutral."

Welch believes that truly great executives don't even have to take their gender into consideration. "They're comfortable with their gender, male or female. They're not going to mask one or the other," he says.

Or could it be that truly great female executives navigate gender differences so instinctively and effectively that the men don't notice?

Donald Trump is another American business legend. Chairman and president of the Trump Organization, his real estate development firm, as well as the founder of Trump Entertainment Resorts, Trump is also the tremendously popular host and executive producer of the NBC reality show *The Apprentice.*

So, does Trump agree with the theory that women executives work harder than men? Trump says that twenty years ago one could make that argument, but not today: "Some of the best people I've ever hired were women," he says. He put a woman in charge of the construction of Trump

Tower, as well as the construction of the Grand Hyatt Hotel in New York, at a time when women in the construction field probably felt they had to try harder in order to prove themselves, he tells me.

"Now I think twenty years ago there was a big difference. There was a theory that women had an inferiority complex when it came to the workplace, right?" Trump says. But that theory doesn't necessarily hold true anymore, because "now when they're really good, they know they're really good."

Could it be that everyone who works for Trump is equally aggressive simply because he hires aggressive people?

"If they're stars I generally find they're aggressive and it doesn't matter whether they're women or men. I hire people who are A types and once they reach a certain level of success, the way they will negotiate with you or talk to you becomes very much the same."

So what makes them successful? What breaks the mold?

Trump says simply, "They have to have drive. Look, you have to start off with the brain. If you don't have the brainpower, the game is over. So let's assume we're dealing with all intelligent people. The one thing that I've seen that separates the really successful people from the people that don't quite get there is the drive. It's that never-ending drive. I went to the Wharton School of Finance, that's the best [business] school, and we had the smartest guys there. I can tell you there were guys in my class who were really smart who never made it because they didn't have the drive."

While I certainly agree with both Welch and Trump that women are equally capable, I have to believe that women bring different abilities and sensibilities to their work, and in many cases that works to their advantage, and to their companies' advantage. Gender research is ongoing, but anecdotal evidence is a powerful thing. All the other women—and men—I spoke with pointed to the fact that women are simply more collaborative.

* * *

"Give me a man and a woman of the same talent, and I will take the woman every single time."
—Donny Deutsch

* * *

"Surrounding myself with women is a real key to my success," Donny Deutsch tells me. Of course he said that! If you've seen Deutsch on *Morning Joe*, you know that we have an ongoing on-air joke about his attitude toward women. He even bought me a pair of $800 shoes to "buy back" my favor after insulting me on air with sarcastic remarks that some regarded as borderline misogynistic. But Deutsch has valuable contributions to make to this conversation. The chairman of a multibillion-dollar advertising agency, he has big money to match his big personality and fancy wardrobe. The man *thinks* big, and he explains how I can too.

"Give me a man and a woman of the same talent, and I will take the woman every single time," he says.

62

Why? He tells me to take a look at advertising: "If you watch little girls in a Saturday morning TV commercial for a Barbie, game, or anything, it's always the same: it's three or four girls sitting around a kitchen table playing together collaboratively—that's the commercial. If you watch a commercial for a little boys' game or toy, at the end one boy always raises his fists: '*I won!*' I think in many ways senior women executives are superior in that for them it's not a zero-sum game. They want to work collaboratively, they want to support, they want to be part of the team. It's not as much how big is my paycheck, how big is my office . . ."

His is a mixed message: on one hand, Deutsch says, yes women may want to be liked, and yes, they do the invisible jobs; that's why he likes women, that's why they are valuable employees. But it is the next words out of his mouth that explain why women so often end up with much of the work and little of the glory: "What I have also found is that—once again, this is not a rule either, there are exceptions to it—but for that very reason sometimes men have made better CEOs because that charge-the-hill aggression, that 'what's in it for me,' the very thing that makes it harder to manage them is what makes them better in the top spot."

I tell Deutsch that there are feminists who are not going to like what he says.

"I'm the ultimate feminist," he fires back. "Eight out of my ten senior partners are women. This is a company I built; the CEO is a woman, the CFO is a woman . . . I'm just saying that some of the time the things that make women more successful in the most senior positions can also work against them."

Although I don't like hearing it, I appreciate Deutsch's honesty. And he's certainly right: women need to get better at charging the hill. I hear essentially the same message from everyone I speak with. Deutsch is simply being generous enough to tell the truth: either we own our value and get to the top, or we can work hard and let the men take the credit.

Most everyone also agreed that women just work harder. Certainly *I* was working as hard as my cohost, and harder than all the other men around me, though I was getting nowhere.

"It's the Fred Astaire–Ginger Rogers thing," Ilene H. Lang says after I recount my story. "Women do the same steps as men, but they do them backwards and in high heels. That's what women have to go through to show that they're as good as men. They have to work harder, they take much longer to be promoted, and they have to prove themselves over and over again."

* * *

"I always felt like I had to be so much better, and in a way that did me a favor."—Susie Essman

* * *

My friend and frequent *Morning Joe* guest Susie Essman may be better known as Susie Green, the foul-mouthed ball-breaking character she plays on the critically acclaimed HBO series *Curb Your Enthusiasm*. But Essman isn't anything like her alter ego Green, who tells her husband to go F himself if she doesn't get what she wants; the real Essman says that despite her success, she is nagged by the feeling that she has to keep proving herself.

Essman has spent most of her career as a stand-up comic. "Talk about a boys' club!" she says of the 1980s New York City comedy circuit. Essman says because the clubs hired mostly men, women had a hard time getting on stage at all, let alone at a decent hour. Women, she says, were often relegated to performing in the wee hours of the morning.

"I always felt like I had to be so much better, and in a way that did me a favor," Essman tells me. "Instead of saying, 'Oh, they're not going to give me a good spot in the clubs because I'm a female,' I was going to be so good they couldn't deny me.

"Was it fair? No. But life isn't fair," Essman says. "I remember that my dad, who was a physician, told me, 'Whenever you go to the doctor, go to a female doctor because they have to work so much harder to get where they are that they're probably better.'"

My favorite senator, Claire McCaskill of Missouri, has spent decades proving herself in the male-dominated world of American politics. When I ask which areas of the economy could benefit from a greater number of women, she tells me, "It is my observation that the women who have done well have been hyperprepared. Being prepared means completely understanding what you're doing. I've always had the feeling someone is going to tap me on the shoulder and say, 'What are you doing here?' So I wanted to be prepared when they did; I wanted to know the answer. And if there's anything that the Wall Street meltdown showed us, it's that a lot of people were engaging in complex financial interactions that they didn't completely understand. My observation is, perhaps if there were more women on board saying, 'Wait a minute, are we sure we understand what this actually is?', then maybe it might have slowed down the train."

There's also the feeling that women, especially when they're in the minority, offer fresh perspective. As I interviewed highly successful women in finance and government, I began to wonder if being in the minority might sometimes work to their advantage.

That's often the case on *Morning Joe.* On days when I'm outnumbered by men, when, for example, Donny Deutsch, Dylan Ratigan, and Lawrence O'Donnell get on a testosterone-fueled roll, I'm the one to say, "Hold on, big boys."

The absence of women in the top spots on Wall Street was blatantly obvious at the height of the financial crisis. If you turned on the television news in the middle of it all, you'll probably recall that iconic scene of the seven heads of the biggest banks hauled before Congress. One couldn't help but notice the total lack of diversity in that line-up.

Some behavioral economists believe there are biological reasons men make crazy bets. Joe Herbert, a neuroscientist at Cambridge University who studied the effects of testosterone on stock traders, told *New York* magazine, "The banking crisis was caused by doing what no society ever allows, permitting young males to behave in an unregulated way. Anyone who studied neurobiology would have predicted disaster."

Headlines such as *New York* magazine's "What If Women Ran Wall Street?" and the *Washington Post's* "In Banking Crisis, Guys Get the Blame, More Women Needed in Top Jobs, Critics Say" promoted the idea that we all might benefit from having more women in positions of power on Wall Street.

Would Wall Street have crumbled in 2008 if women were running the show? I ask both Brooksley Born, former head of the Commodity Futures Trading Commission, and Sheila Bair, current head of the Federal Deposit Insurance Corporation. Both are rarities in the world of government: they've held powerful positions overseeing the banking industry, they famously clashed with Wall Street during their tenure as financial regulators, and both are well-known for displaying political bravery in their (ultimately unsuccessful) attempts to warn the country of looming threats to the American economy. As head of the CFTC during the Clinton administration, Born was among the first to call for greater disclosure and regulation of the rapidly growing market in financial derivatives. As head of the FDIC, the government agency which regulates banks and insures depositors, Sheila Bair has been a prominent figure in the current economic meltdown and was also recognized for her early attempt to get the second Bush administration to address the imminent subprime mortgage crisis.

Neither is willing to categorize women as less likely to be risk takers. Both point to the fact that women in the finance world are outsiders, however, and to some degree that fact helped them bring a new perspective to bear on the industry's problems.

Born says, "You know, I've read these studies about risk taking, but I don't have the expertise to evaluate them. I do think that if you are a bit of an outsider, which certainly a woman in that position [as a government banking regulator] was then, and to some extent is now, you may not be blinded by the conventional wisdom, or the group-think, that is the views held by your peers. You obviously aren't part of the club and therefore don't have pressure to remain in everybody's good graces in quite the same way. Maybe you can analyze things a little independently, and if you come to a different conclusion than the others, maybe you have the courage to express that conclusion."

But the flip side of that coin is, if you're an outsider, nobody's taking you seriously. Born was trained as a lawyer, not a banker, and she acknowledges that that played a role in her inability to force change: "I was not from Wall Street, which many of them were. And in fact, many of them were from the very highest ranks of Wall Street. And that, in and of itself, was a bit of a club, to which I did not belong . . . I also think that they all knew each other to some extent from their previous lives. They didn't know me. I was in a small agency, much smaller than any of the other financial regulatory agencies. It had traditionally been a rather weak agency, a backwater if you will, that happened to oversee derivatives. And in fact, I think [the fact that the agency was a backwater] may have been the reason why, in that era, some women had been head of the CFTC, but no women had been chair of the SEC or of the Fed."

The FDIC's Sheila Bair echoes Born's sentiments. "I do think that to the extent you let outsiders into the financial sector, that's good, and it really is a club world . . . to the extent women have been outsiders, getting them in to take fresh looks and offer fresh perspectives is very helpful." Did being the rare female working in finance put her at a disadvantage when she was calling for reform in the subprime mortgage market? "The media and others have focused on my gender," she explains, "but I think just as relevant is that I am a Midwesterner, and I graduated from a public university, so I was never part of the East Coast, New York financial establishment. I think my frankness was unusual as was my outspokenness, particularly coming from the FDIC, which has historically taken a back seat among financial regulators. While some may have focused on my gender, I think my views may have been too much, too soon for others to adopt them."

I argue that as outsiders in the world of high finance, women like Born and Bair can think more clearly and offer new insights. But in practice, if you're an outsider and nobody's taking your perspective seriously, your insights have no effect because nobody hears you. When I give her my reasoning, Born says, "Exactly. That's the problem!"

Professor Hannah Riley Bowles studies gender in negotiation and leadership at Harvard University. She describes diversity as a double-edged sword: "Diverse teams often perform better than teams that are less diverse," but only if people in the workplace actually value diversity and want to benefit from the fact that dissimilar people will bring alternate experiences and viewpoints to bear on their input. "If you're in a context where people say things like 'diversity doesn't matter, we're really all the same around here, we're color blind, gender blind, or whatever,' then people feel self-conscious about their differences. Then those differences become suppressed, and the potential for communication failures increase," she says, citing research done by Robin Ely and David Thomas at Harvard Business School.

Born's and Bair's unheeded warnings about potentially cataclysmic banking practices could be considered communication failures of the greatest degree.

Obviously there are still major obstacles that keep women from achieving parity in the workplace. But were my own problems caused by gender bias? Have I been discriminated against in my career? Probably, somewhere along the line. But being angry and blaming men (and even high-level women) for holding me back isn't constructive. I take full responsibility, and therefore full credit, for my career. My feeling is, I can only control what I can control. Instead of just being frustrated about the wage disparities that exist in my field, I'd rather think about what I can do within the parameters of my situation. When it came time to take drastic action to resolve my salary problem, I wanted to find ways to take matters into my own hands.

CHAPTER 4

ACCEPTABLE BEHAVIOR
A Cautionary Tale about Women Acting Like Men in the Workplace

MY STORY, WITH DONNY DEUTSCH, HANNAH RILEY BOWLES, JACK WELCH, CAROL BARTZ, JOY BEHAR, SHERYL SANDBERG, SHEILA BAIR, SUSIE ESSMAN, MARIE C. WILSON, AND ARIANNA HUFFINGTON

ACTING LIKE A MAN

For months I had watched Joe cut his own deals and get what he needed for the show. Getting what he wanted meant engaging in loud battles with Phil Griffin on a regular basis. Phil was extremely close to Joe; they had worked together for years.

Often I'd be sitting between them as it began. They'd lean past me and get in each other's face. Invariably the exchange started like this: Joe wants to hire a certain producer or writer or analyst. Phil says no, there is no money. The volume goes up. Then they stand. Then fingers start pointing. There's shouting. Growling. Even threatening. Joe threatening to quit; Phil threatening to fire him. Neither of them meaning it. I watch spit splatter on the coffee table in front of me—I can actually hear it hit the table. *Splat!* As I study the drops, more come raining down.

Soon they get up and stand face-to-face, me sitting awkwardly between them on the couch. They lean in over me, poking each other in the chest, with their faces red and inches apart. Then, as my own stress level escalates to its highest point, there's a miraculous pivot.

One of Joe's talents: diffusing a moment within a blink of an eye.

Joe offers to hug Phil and then fires one last question at him.

"Phil, how the hell can the Mets win the World Series when their pitching is so spotty?"

Phil responds as if the two had been calmly talking sports the whole time. As the spit dries on the table, they sit down and continue with a calm and friendly conversation.

That would never happen with a woman. Never in a million years. No woman could survive a scene like that with her boss. Yet whenever Phil and Joe are negotiating, the drill is the same: they yell, spit, scream, and slam phones down. They each walk away with what they want, and their relationship remains intact. In fact it's better. They'll have something to laugh about later over a beer.

I remember once Phil was screaming, and Joe hung up on him. Phil didn't realize that Joe had hung up so he continued to scream until his assistant knocked on the door and told him that Joe had hung up four minutes ago. Phil was so amused by that that he called Joe back to laugh about it: "F—cker, you wouldn't believe what just happened, I was screaming and you hung up and I didn't know that for four minutes! That's hysterical . . . so what were we talking about? Oh right, yeah sure. I'll give you the extra producer."

After months of watching how Joe's aggressive, in-your-face method seemed to get him what he needed, I decided I'd give it a try.

I went into Phil's office and sat down on his couch and proceeded to tell him in no uncertain terms that my salary was a joke and that he'd better change it.

"I'm really, really tired of not being paid my worth," I said angrily. "You keep saying you will deal with it. When Phil, *when*? This is ridiculous, and I am not going to put up with it anymore." I raised my voice and tossed in a few F-bombs.

The approach was very Joe. Except I am not Joe, and this was not me: my eyes were open a bit too wide; my heart was beating fast, my body shook. My voice rose into the upper register. Higher pitched. Pushing it.

Somehow we ended up standing next to his door, and I was six inches from his face saying something like, "How could you let me be in this position? Seriously Phil, seriously! You need to fix this!" I jabbed him below his left shoulder. Phil jabbed me right back.

I thought, *"Whoa! This is just plain weird."* Phil looked truly alarmed. Our jabs were like awkward pokes.

I wish I could erase this entire scene from my memory, and his. The whole thing was a bad idea. Needless to say, I didn't walk out with a raise. While Joe and many other men could pull this off, I wasn't believable in any way.

Instead, after I left his office, Phil picked up the phone, called Joe and Chris Licht, and asked each of them the same thing: "Motherf—cker, is she crazy?"

That might have been a fair question.

* * *

"We 'bro,' it gets out, and that's it."
—DONNY DEUTSCH

* * *

A *New York Magazine* profile on Donny Deutsch and life at his ad agency described an argument between Deutsch and one of his male employees: "We were screaming. Our noses were touching. Then we started laughing."

I ask Deutsch about that episode, and he explains to me, "We 'bro,' it gets out, and that's it."

So why, I ask incredulously, didn't that work for me?

"Because it was a side Phil wasn't used to seeing. He was threatened, and he didn't know how to handle it," Deutsch answers. "If a women punches you, you don't know what to do. You can't hit a woman back. If she punches you, you think, 'What's wrong with her?'"

Harvard professor Hannah Riley Bowles says another reason my tack did not work is simply that I didn't have the same relationship with Phil that Joe has. "It's generally the case that people tend to know better and hang around with and be closer to people who are like them. Right?" she reasons. "So the implication of that in a male-dominated industry is that guys will tend to be very well connected with guys. Their social network and their work network will tend to be overwhelmingly male." Research done by Herminia Ibarra at INSEAD Business School found that men are more likely to be connected to more senior male executives by virtue of the fact that they're both male. By contrast, women tend to have both male and female colleagues in their work networks, but their networks of close friends are likely to be mostly women and friends from outside of work. "So if you have someone who is a friend and a colleague, you can speak to them and relate to them in ways that you cannot with someone with whom you have a more distant, or just really collegial, relationship," Bowles tells me. She says the difference is that in a male-dominated industry, men typically develop both work ties and friendship ties at work, and "You can communicate differently with someone with whom you have work and friendship ties than with whom you just have work ties."

* * *

"Authenticity is a huge deal."—Jack Welch

* * *

I decide to ask former CEO of General Electric, business guru Jack Welch why he thinks my approach backfired so badly. He argues that women make a mistake when they try to mimic what they see men do. "Authenticity is a huge deal," he said, for both women and men. "Men are jerks when they're not themselves . . . I mean authenticity is a killer, and women sometimes don't behave as themselves," he says.

For most women, an aggressive verbal style is just out of character. Yahoo CEO Carol Bartz may be the exception. Known for her fearless leadership style as well as her willingness to use foul language, she says, "Well, I mean, listen, this business that goes on about my 'salty language' . . . come on, there are men who could run my language into the ground and nobody cares. Yes, I am an outspoken person; I have been probably for the last twenty years. As I earned the right, I got more outspoken. I just developed a style that works for me, and I think it's authentic. I just met with a lot of the interns, and I said you can't copy me because a) you haven't earned the right, and b) if it's not comfortable, everybody can see that."

For the rest of us who aren't comfortable with it, strong language only backfires. A lot of people I consulted with agree that the problem wasn't really what I said, it was my delivery. I just wasn't being authentic with Phil. But what about the fact that I was *authentically* angry? Hannah Riley Bowles comments, "Even if you were genuinely pissed, if you were acting like a guy, it probably wouldn't work. There is a lot of evidence, our research included, that adopting the guys' style of doing this is likely to be risky for women. When women just act like the guys, then they pay really important social costs."

Bowles and other researchers have various names for this problem. They call it the double bind, or the backlash effect. Research shows that assertiveness is an important quality for leadership. But when women are assertive, it can hurt them, because being assertive is not an appealing trait in women.

Professors Frank Flynn, Cameron Anderson, and Sebastien Brion tested this effect on a group of business students at New York University. MBA students were asked to read a Harvard Business School case about a very successful Silicon Valley entrepreneur by the name of Heidi Roizen.

The case is often used to teach students networking skills, but the researchers decided to use the case for a study on gender and bias. They gave half their students the case under the real name of Heidi Roizen and the other half a case about "Howard Roizen." The cases were exactly the same, except for a couple of descriptive words: Heidi's "husband" was changed to Howard's "wife," and Heidi the "cheerleader" became Howard the "football player." Both Heidi and Howard were described in assertive terms as take-charge executives, captains of industry.

After reading over the case, the students went online to answer questions about their impressions of Heidi/Howard. They were asked to rate him or her on characteristics such as kindness, generosity, ambition, manipulativeness, concern for others, and a variety of other typically gender-associated traits.

The results were shocking. The students were looking at exactly the same information, but they rated Heidi less kind and less generous than Howard and more power hungry, manipulative, and assertive than Howard. Clearly the students responded negatively to Heidi's aggressiveness.

When the students were asked whether they would want to work with Howard and whether they'd hire Heidi, the researchers discovered that both men and women thought Heidi was competent, but less likeable. Heidi may have been a little full of herself, but Howard was the kind of guy they'd go have a beer with.

The double bind is this: in order to be a competent leader you need to be assertive—but if you're a woman, you're judged harshly for displaying the traits that make you an effective leader.

I wasn't surprised to hear that the data showed men were more critical of women than of other men. But I *was* surprised that women were equally critical of both genders. Women are as hard on each other as they are on themselves.

Flynn's students insisted that they didn't judge Heidi any differently. After the test was completed, however, Flynn shared the results with them, and they, too, were shocked. Flynn says that confronting this group with their own subconscious bias was a powerful lesson for them all. When Flynn relayed the results to the real Heidi Roizen, she responded, "Well, I guess that's understandable, with a group of grizzled executives." She was as surprised as anyone to learn the test subjects were twenty-six-year-old MBA students.

OUR ACHILLES' HEEL

The simple fact is that even the most successful women among us just want to be liked. Joy Behar is not comfortable being a bitch. Yes, I said that. Like Susie Essman, Behar rose up the ranks in the world of stand-up comedy. Currently she's on television two hours each day, hosting her own talk show as well as *The View*. She is both unfailingly funny and searingly blunt. During the 2008 campaign, Behar famously asked John McCain some of the toughest questions he faced. He arrived on set of *The View*, no doubt expecting light conversation, when Behar confronted him on his campaign commercials: "We know that those two ads are untrue, they are lies. And yet, you at the end of it say you approve these messages. Do you really approve them?"

This is a woman who doesn't have a hard time speaking her mind, so it might surprise you to learn that she doesn't speak up when it comes to asking for money and perks. "I'm just a big mouth," Behar tells me, "[but] I'm not demanding, and I don't say I have to get special privileges or anything like that." It's not that she doesn't want the big money and the big perks; it's just that, like most women, being demanding makes her uncomfortable. "You want people to feel that you're a team player," she says. "I've always been the good girl, in a certain way. I have always been the good team player."

Plus, there's the risk that she'll be called a bitch. But don't bitches often get what they want? "The squeaky wheel gets the grease, as they say," Behar says. "They don't really give a f—k that you think that they're a bitch. You and I, we don't like to be thought of as bitches . . . if you don't care that people think you're a bitch, you can run the networks and the country. I don't have that; I'm not comfortable with being a bitch."

Behar is right. I didn't want to be thought of as the b-word. And that was the crux of my problem: I really wanted to be liked.

My desire to be liked outweighed my wish to be valued. When my bosses would compliment me for being "a jack-of-all-trades," a warm feeling rushed over me. I felt . . . liked. But I have learned the hard way that compliments don't pay the bills. Which brings me back to my story, and one of the best and worst moments of my career, all at the same time.

NEW HAMPSHIRE AND THE RED HAIR CLIP

New Hampshire was pivotal in the run-up to Super Tuesday. This primary would decide whether Hillary Clinton, whose candidacy was on the rocks, would drop her bid for the presidency. Instead it turned out to be the place she "found her voice." But before she did, we found her at 9:30 at night on a high school stage in Nashua. We had been trying to get some time with her all day. My phone did not leave my ear and we did not get out of the car until we nailed down the interview.

Everyone was predicting a crushing loss for Hillary. But the Hillary we saw that night was a winner. As usual, she had been up earlier than everyone and she stayed up later, fighting both the odds and her critics. She was unflappable. Determined. Confident. Hair perfect. Makeup intact.

We walked away from our interview in awe of her physical might and resilience. How was she still going? This is when Joe Scarborough's adoration for "his girlfriend" Hillary Rodham Clinton began. He started to say it every day on the air:

"I can't deny it. My girlfriend is tougher than any man I've met on the campaign trail."

She is a force of nature, and clearly when the chips are down, Hillary Clinton is at her very best. To this day, both Joe and I think she was by far the strongest candidate in terms of steel will and political agility. When she won the next day, her surprise victory made for an incredible narrative.

Late into the night, we discussed how impressed we were and what it would mean for the race if she didn't drop out. We were still buzzing about the interview we had worked so hard to get. Joe and I had scrambled across the country by car and by plane and had to be on the air the next morning for another grueling six hours . . . But we didn't care how tired we were. We had the story and a great show to tell it on.

The next day, after the interview aired, my phone rang. I saw it was an NBC line, and I assumed I was going to be given kudos for the Hillary get—maybe I would be closer to getting that raise. They must have heard how hard we worked, how I didn't give up until we got that interview. How we hadn't slept in days but still found a way to nail the story. The interview was aired over and over again on MSNBC and then again on *NBC Nightly News*. So this must be one of our bosses calling with a pat on the back.

Uh, not quite.

I picked up the phone and heard, "Hello, Mika? What was with that clip in your hair last night? Do not wear that clip again. You looked awful, don't ever wear that clip in your hair again. Seriously, you looked like a cancer survivor. That clip is awful. I am trying to help you here. You can't do it again. I want people to like you."

It's true that when we had caught up with Hillary the night before, Joe and I were both in jeans and winter boots and ragged from days on the road and spending six hours straight on-air each day. I had thrown my hair up in a plastic hair clip that I'd gotten at a drugstore, and my makeup had pretty much worn off. I was beginning to be comfortable traveling with the guys. Just like them, I let the "real me" hang out. When we were under the gun, I simply couldn't look camera-ready at all times. The guys were great and told me not to bother with makeup. That it shouldn't matter so much. That it would be better to show my real side anyway. That is what our show was about. I could be me.

NBC obviously disagreed.

How did I respond to the call?

I apologized.

Again, this is a story of what *not* to do. Why didn't I simply hang up? That's what Joe would have done. Surely that's what Hillary Clinton would've done! I should have been crystal clear and defiant. I had scored a major victory—that's what the manager should've taken away from that piece. I felt powerful; I *was* powerful. But I didn't take the opportunity to set her straight.

I'm sure we both would have been better off had I spoken up. We still might not have agreed on the hair clip, but I would have earned her respect, and I would have had the satisfaction of explaining that she'd missed the point: the important thing here was that we'd gotten a key interview on the most exciting night of the election season thus far. This was the stuff of great television.

In the weeks that followed, my exchange with the manager about the damn hair clip stayed with me. Would it have been such a big deal if I'd pushed back? Was I afraid of sounding like a bitch? The answer was probably yes. I realized that wanting to be liked was really getting in my way. But when I took a more aggressive tack and decided that raising my voice and poking Phil Griffin in the shoulder would get me somewhere—well, we know how well that worked out. So where was the middle ground? How was I ever going to be both likeable and fairly compensated?

"How women can do both, get what they want materially and also make a positive social image" is a tricky thing to pull off, says Professor Hannah Riley Bowles. "I think it's flawed to say that women need to be trained to negotiate more assertively or that they need more confidence to close the gender gap in negotiation performance." Because clearly, women who are assertive suffer a backlash, so it's entirely reasonable for them to be reticent about asking for what they want.

Bowles tells me that there's no easy solution. Women have to be strategic and come up with their own way of asking for higher pay. "One strategy that we have found to be effective is what we call using a 'relational account.' This involves explaining why the negotiating request is legitimate in terms that inherently communicate concern for organizational relationships." They have to find a feminine way of getting what they deserve, because negotiating for something like higher compensation in its essence "contradicts what you're supposed to be like as a woman. Giving, not taking; generous, not materialistic . . . it contradicts a lot of expectations we hold for women consciously or unconsciously."

Walking that tightrope of acceptable behavior leaves women in a quandary.

* * *

"Downplay, downplay, downplay."
—SHERYL SANDBERG

* * *

Facebook COO Sheryl Sandberg agrees that there's a very good reason why women don't own their success: because success and likeability are positively correlated for men and negatively correlated for women. Says Sandberg: "It makes sense that women behave as they do in the workplace. It's not irrational behavior; it's rational behavior not to own our success. That's the point. It would be easier if the answer were to tell everyone just to start negotiating more. But it's not so easy, because it's not necessarily going to work. Just like what happened to you, it backfires."

Sandberg has two young children, and when I ask her how she handles the dual roles of motherhood and executive, she says, "I'll tell you what I always say: I do everything badly. No man ever says that, by the way, that's what *we* say." (In fact, as Sandberg and I talk further about work-life balance, I exclaim, "You're amazing!" Her automatic response: "I'm really not." She's nothing if not consistent.)

Sandberg's guiding principle for successful women: "Downplay, downplay, downplay."

But then the question is, if women have to continually downplay their success, if they aren't aggressive about getting paid what they're worth, how do they get anywhere? Obviously there have to be times when you don't soft-pedal your success, when you need to step up and be heard. Again, we have to find our own path.

That's exactly the advice Donny Deutsch gives me when I bemoan the fact that women are punished both for being too aggressive and for not being aggressive enough: "I think there's a middle ground," he says. "I think it's about being smart. The answer is understanding those two sides of the coin. Saying I'm going to be firm, I'm going to be direct, I'm still managing up to a weaker sex, women managing men, in order to get what I want. I'm not going to challenge them to a duel, but I'm not going to be passive and I'm not going to use 'please' and 'thank you' and all that stuff. It's doing it with a softer touch, but with that same level of firepower and that's the difference."

FINDING THE MIDDLE GROUND: NOT TOO SOFT, NOT TOO HARD

The experiences of women in male-dominated industries illustrate on a larger scale the hurdles women face every day. When I met Sheila Bair, chair of the FDIC, for a sit-down interview for this book, my stomach was in knots. In 2009, *Forbes* named Bair the second most powerful woman in the world for the role she played in handling the financial crisis. I wondered if a woman who was dealing with the momentous problems facing our economy on a regular basis would be able to relate at all to my career issues. I was stunned at how much we had common. Soon we were chuckling together over the similarities of our struggles, despite the difference in our fields.

* * *

"Don't ever get emotional."—SHEILA BAIR

* * *

I ask Bair to give examples of the strategies she uses to make her way through the male bastion of finance.

"Emotionalism doesn't work," Bair tells me. "Don't ever get emotional. Sometimes that's hard. You get so frustrated and you care deeply. I'm the kind of person who cares deeply, but emotionalism never works. It always has the opposite effect."

I ask, "Did you ever get emotional?"

"There were probably a couple of times during the bailout discussions . . ." Bair answers.

"Are we talking about tears?" I ask.

"No, it never got that far," she says. "I'm really talking more about anger; for me it was more anger. When you're angry it hurts your ability to think straight. If you start to get angry, the adrenaline starts pumping in you."

"If no one is listening to you, how do you *not* get angry?" I ask.

"Frankly, I think that just takes a lot of maturity to deal with, and I've gotten better at it over the years. You just have to control yourself. If you let yourself respond with anger or with emotion, it's going to make things worse, not better, and you'll suffer a loss of respect."

"Can a man get angry?" I ask.

"Yes, and they even get angry with each other," Bair says, "and it doesn't seem to do anything at all. But if we get angry with them it doesn't work, it backfires. I've witnessed men at my level go at each other on occasion, and that's just accepted, even by the press." If she had growled in a similar way she would've been labeled an emotional woman.

I ask Bair if being too assertive has backfired for her, the way it did for me when I tried to get a raise.

"With certain personalities, yes, it can," she answers. "I think it's unfortunate that sometimes being assertive doesn't work, where being helpless works or being flattering works. I say that because I try to be a good person and not a disingenuous person, but I recognize that certain strategies work. I think sometimes it makes them feel they're in control; I'm sorry—it does. It prevents them from feeling threatened by your argument if you're coming to them for help: 'I have this idea. Advise me how we can move this forward. Is this a good idea?' You know, sometimes that approach works better. It does. It can be disarming in a way that produces results without being threatening."

That's right. The chairman of the FDIC suggests flattery. I was both surprised and amused.

And I suspect many women reading this may roll their

eyes. But I went on to hear the same advice from women as different as Carol Bartz and Susie Essman.

Yahoo CEO Carol Bartz agrees that the best way to get men to listen is to compliment them. She tells me about an economic summit she was invited to when Bill Clinton was running for president. She claims that she was invited "because, you know, they had to have so many skirts," but then she was promptly ignored. "I walked in and nobody would pay any attention to me. They would shake my hand and be looking over my shoulder, obviously trying to see if there was somebody much more important behind me. I found that I finally had to start by saying, 'Oh, I've always admired you so much,' you know . . . *blah, blah, blah,* even to be able to engage with any of the men."

Basically, Bartz tells me, "You just do what you have to, to fit in."

Comedian and actress Susie Essman tells me that one of the advantages that women have over men is that we have better people skills. We don't need to be aggressive, because we have methods of manipulation that are far more effective. "One of my strategies is always to play to men's narcissism in a way that is so subtle they don't know what hit them. I think we have to use our wiles," she says. "When I say *feminine wiles,* I don't mean sexual. I mean . . . we're a completely different species, men and women. I think that we have to recognize those differences. I do believe that women are—I don't want to say smarter—but we're more well-rounded. There are all these articles they're writing now about how women are better CEOs than men because they're more conciliatory. In life it's worked really well for me to be really conciliatory but strong at the same time. It's a balance. We are fence menders. We build relationships and building relationships is the way to go."

A number of women I interviewed agreed that flattery is the way to go, but not necessarily flirting. They're not the same thing. If the person on the receiving end is a man, however, being complimentary may be interpreted as flirting. Hannah Riley Bowles warns that "The data out on flirting—research done by Laura Kray at UC Berkeley—is not that encouraging. Flirting tends to make you appealing, but not particularly persuasive." So here again, women have to walk a very fine line.

HARD AS NAILS, WARM AS TOAST

Women's advocate Marie C. Wilson echoed what others have said, that when women play hardball and negotiate like a man, they just don't get the same response that a man would. She says the people who teach negotiation, like Professor Linda Babcock at Carnegie Mellon, observe that when women go in to negotiate, they have to do it by being "relentlessly pleasant." We still carry our own stereotypes about what women are supposed to be like, and yet when you go in to negotiate for a raise, "It's hard to remember that as a woman you have to go negotiate with a big smile on your face," she says.

There really are different expectations for behavior. Does Wilson envision a time when women won't have to negotiate differently than men? Yes. Wilson believes all of that will change when the numbers shift, and women outnumber men in the workplace—or at least surpass that magic one-third.

"But until that happens, women walk a fine line," Wilson says. "Because, as my friend Anna Quindlen says, women 'have to be tough as nails *and* warm as toast.' . . . You get penalized when you take either one of those positions separately. If you go in and you're apologetic, you know, you're toast. If you go in and you do it in a way that's tough as nails, then you're hammered. You have to go in and do it in a way that is relentlessly pleasant."

Many of the people I spoke with believe that more women are in positions of power, and if more people (both men and women) are made aware of their own unconscious biases, that women will be able to be assertive in the workplace with fewer repercussions. Until then, we figure it out as we go.

Journalist and *Huffington Post* cofounder Arianna Huffington knows very well the potential social risk of being a powerful woman. "The most important thing for women is not to internalize the attacks on them, and to realize that any time they speak out they are going to have attacks leveled at them," she advises. "Let's face it: our culture still isn't comfortable with outspoken women. As Marlo Thomas famously put it, 'A man has to be Joe McCarthy to be called ruthless. All a woman has to do is put you on hold.'" Huffington says that she finds the best way to neutralize this kind of attitude is through humor and perspective.

"Too often in our culture, strong women get stereotyped as ball-busters, which is as insulting as it is ludicrous,"

Huffington tells me. "In my experience, the strongest, most fearless women I know are also the most creative and productive—and the ones who most want to support other women. And, honestly, wouldn't any healthy man really prefer to be involved with a woman—either personally or professionally—who is driven by her true thoughts, feelings, beliefs, and desires instead of her fears?"

The fact is, there just aren't enough female role models. As Hannah Riley Bowles points out, "The high-powered female executive is really a new phenomenon, and these women are creating what that person is as they're doing it." Men have plenty of role models when they're looking for examples of people in the highest leadership positions. "Women do have to come up with their own ways of doing these things," she says.

So if acting like a man didn't get me anywhere, what strategies should I have used instead?

CHAPTER 5

WHAT MEN KNOW
We Can't Act Like Them, but We Can Learn from Them

MY STORY, WITH CHRYSTIA FREELAND, ARIANNA HUFFINGTON, KATE WHITE, ELIZABETH WARREN, SUZE ORMAN, SHEILA BAIR, DONNY DEUTSCH, VALERIE JARRETT, CAROL BARTZ, BROOKSLEY BORN, AND JACK WELCH

FINDING OUR OWN WAY

My own experience, and now the experiences shared by so many other women in these pages, convinces me that women can't act like men and expect to be liked, to be able to lead, and to be paid what they're worth. But we still need to accomplish all of those goals. Reuters' global editor-at-large Chrystia Freeland notes, "We as women are still immigrants; we don't speak the native language very well. It might not be that these male ways of behaving are, absent other factors, better, but they are the dominant cultural mode, and like all immigrants we have to conform to the dominant cultural mode. We can learn a lot from the men around us."

Surely our demeanor and delivery have to be different,

and that's our main challenge. *Huffington Post* cofounder Arianna Huffington describes the situation succinctly: "In order to conquer the workplace as women, we need to approach it in our own unique way, not as carbon copies of men: briefcase-carrying, pinstripe-wearing career machines who just happen to have vaginas." The way to get ahead? Huffington answers, "By learning how to play the men's office 'game,' but tailoring it to our own style."

A SENSE OF ENTITLEMENT

In addition to a career as the author of bestselling mysteries and thrillers such as *Hush* as well as nonfiction books such as *Why Good Girls Don't Get Ahead but Gutsy Girls Do*, Kate White is the editor-in-chief of *Cosmopolitan* magazine. She has many stories to tell about what women in the workplace could learn from men.

* * *

"Some of the guys I've worked with have just had a really great sense of entitlement."
—KATE WHITE

* * *

When she was the editor of *Working Woman* magazine, White hired a guy—let's call him Jack—as a senior editor. There were three other senior editors, all women. When Jack was first hired, all the editors had their own offices, but soon, for economic reasons, the magazine moved into a new building with less space. "It turned out that all four senior editors were going to have to work out of this big room that had once been the company library," she says. White knew this would not go over well. "I went down to see what was happening, and discovered that Jack had slipped some money to the movers when all the furniture was being delivered," she tells me. "He arranged for them to give him a big old bookcase, which he used to divide off his area, and then he got them to bring up a little couch from the basement. Brilliant. Suddenly he had an office. If you had walked in you would have thought he was the boss and the three women were in the typing pool. He just said to himself, 'Okay, this isn't the best situation. What do I have to do to fix it to my advantage?'"

White says many women think, " 'Hey, we're following orders here, we're doing what we're supposed to do,' whereas a lot of guys in the workplace make up the rules as they go along. Men scam the situation . . . Jack had an air of entitlement that said, 'I deserve this, and I'm going to get it.' I just laughed and thought, 'What can I learn from this guy?'"

She's right; a woman's tendency is to fall in line and accept the status quo, even if it doesn't benefit her. Women seem more willing to be accommodating than to insist on being accommodated.

* * *

"Someone needs to do this. Someone needs to mop the floor. Okay, hand me the mop."
—Elizabeth Warren

* * *

Morning Joe regular guest Elizabeth Warren is a Harvard law professor. In September 2010 she was appointed Assistant to the President and Special Advisor to the Secretary of the Treasury on the Consumer Financial Protection Bureau, a position in which she will build the new agency that will oversee the rules on financial products such as mortgages and credit cards. She's a woman who surely would be horrified by all the mistakes I've made along the way in my career, or so I thought.

As a longtime advocate for consumers, Warren has gone up against some of the biggest names on Wall Street, and she has famously locked horns with Treasury Secretary Tim Geithner. Warren, who has been on *Time* magazine's list of the World's Most Influential People for two years running and often appears on our show to talk about the economy and financial reform, impresses me as a sharp, gutsy, no-nonsense woman. But she admits to me that when it comes to her personal value in the workplace, she still struggles.

Warren remembers how surprised she was when she realized her male colleagues had that sense of entitlement that she lacked. It happened when she first started teaching at the University of Houston. Before the semester began, she heard from the associate dean, who was scheduling courses. "I got the call asking, 'Would you teach the lousy course at the lousy hour on the lousy day in the lousy room?'" she says. She didn't want to teach that particular class, but she didn't see any way around it: "I thought, I'm sure someone needs to teach at the lousy hour on the lousy day in the lousy room, so I said, 'I'll do it.'"

A couple of years later, Warren was promoted to associate dean, and it was now her job to assign courses, classrooms, and time slots. "So I took the map from the year before and started laying it out, and I sent all these notes out on what and when I needed people to teach," she remembers. "But every single man on the faculty who didn't like their schedule sent me back an e-mail saying, 'You know, you don't understand, I only teach at ten o'clock on Mondays, Tuesdays, and Wednesdays.'"

And the women?

Warren says, "Every single woman could be leveraged into teaching the lousy course at the lousy time in the lousy room. Men would just say, 'No. That's not convenient for me.' I thought, 'This is astonishing!'"

I ask Warren, "It never crossed your mind to say no?"

"Never," Warren says.

"Why?"

"Partly I felt lucky to be there; partly, I'm the cooperator, you know, let's get the job done. Someone needs to do this. Someone needs to mop the floor. Okay, hand me the mop. I really see this as the difference between putting ourselves, if not first, at least putting equivalent value on ourselves . . . we don't see our own worth. We see how we can be helpful to the team or to the group. We see what we can add without stopping to ask, 'Wait a minute, this is a valuable contribution— why am I making this, and what am I getting in return for it?'

"You're always careful about generalizations here, but for me it doesn't even cross my mind until later, when I'm committed to do something and I suddenly look around and realize, 'So how come the three people who agreed to do the hard, invisible labor here are all women?'"

Warren points out that while the low-profile jobs may be both necessary and important, they just don't garner the accolades or the money and promotions. For that reason, men simply never pick up the mop. She sees this at her faculty meetings at Harvard. "Someone will say, 'Well, you know we should hire X because he . . .' and they will name three very visible accomplishments. And I know for a fact, and every woman in the room knows for a fact, that X is a real pain in the rear: X won't cooperate, won't help out, won't be a team player. X will not help move the whole institution forward, and that's regarded as irrelevant. You know, it's the difference between the big valuable things that people do, and all that stuff that women do—that's all that crap stuff. That's the stuff no one notices, no one cares. No one values."

I can think of countless lousy shifts that I've volunteered to work in my life. Time away from my husband and my kids, time that I needed to take care of myself, that I gave up in order to work. To be the cooperator, the person with the mop. I know for a fact those lost hours made no difference to my employers, but it is the lost time with my family that I'll never get back. I often pushed my self to extremes to get nothing in return except bad health, and at one point, a baby with a broken leg. Warren's description of herself when she was starting out made me cringe, because that was me. Always trying to run faster, to please everyone, and very seldom getting anything in return.

IF YOU'RE NOT PAID FOR IT, DON'T DO IT

Personal-finance expert and force of nature Suze Orman argues that for their own sake, women have to resist the urge to always pick up the mop. When you know what you're worth, you'll have an easier time asking to be compensated for what you're bringing to the job. And if you're not getting paid for it, take a lesson from men and don't do it.

"I know my own worth and I'm not going to settle for less," Orman says. "It's really just that simple. When I'm giving my speaking lectures, I get exactly what I want for my speaking lectures, and if you can't pay me, then I'm not going to speak for you. I get exactly what I want from CNBC, and I'm very happy. I don't have to demand; you either give it to me or you don't. If you don't, then it's not my problem."

Of course, at this point in her career, it's easy for Suze Orman to say no. She acknowledges that in the current recession, most people don't have that luxury. Most people do what they have to do, and sometimes, that does include picking up the mop and even working for free. "When you're first working for someone, your goal is to make those people whom you are dependent on dependent on you," Orman advises. "So when you first start working, you do not demand anything, you do not ask for anything. That's when you do everything you can, even if you're not asked to do it. You make them totally dependent on you—and then you've reversed the power." When you really need the money, or the opportunity, sometimes you do have to get your foot in the door and take the lousy shift. But once you've made yourself essential, that's when you have leverage. It's up to you to make sure your boss sees your contribution and knows you expect to be paid for it.

Orman says she sometimes worked for free as she worked her way up. She worked unpaid the entire first year of her show, because she and her managers weren't able to settle on contract terms. But at the end of the first year she had proven herself and was in an excellent negotiating position. At this writing, her show is in its tenth year.

BE VISIBLE—AND WILLING TO PROMOTE YOURSELF

FDIC chair Sheila Bair told me that while she hasn't haggled over the issue of compensation, she has certainly felt at times that her opinions have not been valued: "Traditionally women's work or opinions or both have not been valued as much as they should. The societal notion that women's work or opinions are less valuable can seep into our own thinking. Perhaps on a subconscious level, but I think it does seep in. We can be accepting of what we get and not ask for more and not think that we deserve more. I think that goes from compensation, office space, titles, to getting credit for saying something and making it your idea. Somehow it's a bad thing to stand up for yourself or promote yourself . . . to speak up and say, 'I deserve to be paid X,' and we feel embarrassed or ashamed or bashful about that, and we shouldn't."

* * *

"The societal notion that women's work or opinions are less valuable can seep into our own thinking."—SHEILA BAIR

* * *

Bair told me she thinks women need to be more assertive. She says we need to educate our managers about our worth: "When there is unequal treatment, learn how to promote yourself in a way that is constructive. You don't have to be obnoxious about it; you can be factual about it. You say, 'This is my idea,' and don't back down. Say it, and don't be embarrassed by saying it."

Advertising exec Donny Deutsch says that for men, keeping track of accomplishments is as natural as breathing. "Men grow up playing games and keeping score from the time they're four years old, and that continues in the workplace. Keeping score by tracking how much money you make, how big your office is, what are the perks, what do other people think, how does it look."

Deutsch says all that scorekeeping makes male employees high maintenance. "I've found without exception that for every alpha male who has worked for me, I've had to spend a lot more time negotiating literally and figuratively . . . the size of everything. For them it's, 'I want more; what's in it for me?'"

Women may not need or want to keep calling attention

to themselves, but as Obama adviser Valerie Jarrett put it, "If you're not negotiating the size of everything, odds are, you're not going to become the boss." Because as I pointed out, even if we don't care about nice offices or elevated titles, the rest of the world does recognize those symbolic stature-oriented achievements.

BEING VISIBLE HAS ITS DRAWBACKS, BUT SO WHAT?

News of Carol Bartz's compensation was splashed across the front pages of newspapers across the country when she got the job as Yahoo CEO in 2009. Bartz says she found it "absolutely fascinating" how reports exaggerated her pay, calling her 'the highest-paid *whatever*,' which is such bullshit because if they really read the fine print, they'd see the stock price has to go up, the moon has to be full and cats have to howl and so forth," before she'd get her full compensation package.

* * *

"First I got mad, and then I got embarrassed, and then I said, 'You know what? Not my problem.'"
—CAROL BARTZ

* * *

But what bothered her most was "the sheer embarrassment of the scrutiny." Everyone was coming up to my husband and saying, 'Well, I guess you can afford a new set of clubs,' and, you know, razzing him. People were putting copies of articles in his locker. It was just bizarre. First I got mad, and then I got embarrassed, and then I said, 'You know what? Not my problem.' I'm proud of this, and if some young woman thinks she can be 'the highest-paid whatever,' then good!"

Why are we afraid to be called self-promoting, and why wouldn't we feel great about being "the highest-paid whatever"? Maybe we feel as if we're being set up to be knocked down or that people think we're only in it for the money. Or maybe the fact that people notice that we're highlighting our accomplishments distracts from the accomplishments themselves?

In her experience as a law professor and in her government positions as chairwoman of TARP and now the chief advisor in charge of setting up the Consumer Financial Protection Bureau, Elizabeth Warren knows that to be labeled self-promoting may not be a bad thing for a man, but it is for a woman: "It's like having something sort of deeply wrong about you. You sense this is a really bad thing."

* * *

"The notion that I'm self-promoting somehow makes me gasp."—ELIZABETH WARREN

* * *

Warren has spent years advocating for consumer protections in the financial-services industry, and she was often interviewed by reporters covering the financial crisis. She has taken a lot of flak from those who don't like her views, and she told me she understood that that came with the territory. But when the *Wall Street Journal* called her "self-promoting," she says that she felt transported back to her childhood in Oklahoma, suddenly feeling like an odd girl out. She remembers thinking, "'Oh my god, I do so much less press than I'm asked to do, and when I do it I always try to do it in the service of trying to teach something, trying to advance an idea' . . . it really stung."

Warren continues: "You know, when someone says, 'Oh, she's just plain stupid,' it doesn't cut to the quick. It doesn't undermine me in the same way. It doesn't even throw me off. But the notion that I'm self-promoting somehow makes me gasp." She says that finally, after two years of working in a much more public position, she's developed thicker skin and the ability to stop and think, "'Wait a minute. Why does that one cut to the quick?' I think more than once I've wondered, 'Would you say that if I were a man?'"

SPEAK UP, AND MAKE SURE YOUR IDEAS ARE HEARD

"I've been in a room countless times where I had said something and no one said anything, no one paid attention. Then a man has said the exact same thing, and people have listened," Valerie Jarrett tells me. "It hasn't happened to me in this White House, but it's happened to me countless times in the past. I think that every woman has experienced that. I don't know whether it's the way we speak it, or if it's because we're women and people have discounted what we said. I can think of many, many times when I've said something and it's been overlooked."

Study after study has documented this phenomenon. And woman after woman told me she had experienced some version of it. But for women to achieve their value, they have to find a way to be heard. Nowhere has that been more difficult and more public than on Wall Street, where a few women have dared to go up against an army of powerful men.

* * *

"What was frustrating was that they wouldn't even engage."—SHEILA BAIR

* * *

FDIC chair Sheila Bair was one of the first people to raise concerns about problems with the subprime mortgage market. She famously battled the "men in charge" of the various regulatory agencies. She tells me it was often difficult to get her counterparts to listen. It was probably for a variety of reasons, including the FDIC's traditionally conservative philosophy and posture. "I become frustrated when people won't even engage," she says. "If you're not going to agree with me, tell me why you don't agree with me and let me respond to that. Don't just nod and smile and go off and don't do anything. So that's really frustrating, and I think that's the first hurdle: at least getting people to engage—even if they're going to disagree with you or not accept your views, at least get them to listen and have a give and take. You have to keep coming back at them and demand a response to your views."

When I press Bair for an instance she would be willing to share in which she felt her ideas were ignored, she refers me to a series of public incidents in 2007. At the time, the mortgage market was starting to go south, and Bair was pushing for a federal program that would encourage banks to modify loans for millions of homeowners. The idea was to lower payments and extend the length of the mortgages so families could remain in their homes, keep the mortgages performing, and head off an epidemic of foreclosures.

Bair was initially unable to convince Treasury Secretary Hank Paulson or the Bush White House to support the program. But then Governor Arnold Schwarzenegger decided to launch a loan modification project in California modeled on her plan. When Schwarzenegger adopted the project, he gave the idea additional credibility, and Hank Paulson saw its merits. "He came around . . . and it provided some momentum for the administration to say, 'Okay, if Arnold is doing it, it must be a good idea.' So then we did it on a federal level."

Like Brooksley Born and Sheila Bair, Elizabeth Warren talks about the "profound insularity on Wall Street." She says, "The guys who ran it were guys who talked only to each other and valued only each other. That was their downfall. They didn't want to hear the evidence that said, 'Your game doesn't work. Your plan is broken' . . . and so it was, you know, '*Lalalala*, we can't hear you.'"

* * *

"I've picked the girls' end of the discussion."
—ELIZABETH WARREN

* * *

Warren's work has an effect on Wall Street and corporate America. She told me that she works in "a field in which male voices dominate almost exclusively."

Warren says she was not just in the minority because she's a woman but also because she has taken the "girls' side" of finance: "I want to talk about the consumer impact of much of what Wall Street does, and in many circles that makes it doubly unpopular. You know, I've picked the girls' end of the discussion . . . because the cool stuff, the guys' stuff, is to talk about leveraged buyouts and credit-default swaps.

"I've been in groups of academics and we're talking about financial innovation, and everyone in the room wanted to talk about [mortgage-backed securities and collateralized debt obligations], and when I would raise my hand to say, 'The first problem with financial innovation has been the families . . . the thirty-page credit card agreements and mortgages . . . there's just a long dead silence, and finally someone says, 'Well, yes, but we only talk about the things that have a really important impact.'

"I know what all that means and I can talk about it. We can sit here and have back-and-forth on theoretical ideas and what the data show, but the part that has been missing from the conversation is the impact on families . . . that the raw materials for much of the financial bubble and crash were people's home mortgages and credit card agreements. We know that now, but no one wanted to talk about this three years ago."

* * *

"If I respect you, I will disagree with you. If I don't respect you, I'll just say you don't understand."
—ELIZABETH WARREN

* * *

Despite resistance, Warren continued to voice her concerns. And she suffered a backlash, in a very public way.

She remembers the litany: "'Doesn't have the right background, doesn't play the political game, doesn't understand how things are done' . . . for which there's a little voice in me that always said, 'Oh, no, I understand; I just think it's wrong.' . . . The whole game is 'doesn't understand' rather than 'we just disagree.' You know, people need to show respect to disagree with you: if I respect you, I will disagree with you. If I don't respect you, I'll just say you don't understand."

* * *

"How many men are called *strident*?"
—BROOKSLEY BORN

* * *

Perhaps the best example of this backlash came a decade before the economy faltered, when another female regulator,

110

Brooksley Born, went up against Wall Street. Born was the chair of the Commodity Futures Trading Commission (CFTC). In the late 1990s, she warned of the risk from the credit default swaps and other financial time bombs that would eventually cause the economic collapse. But nobody listened.

Born's agency wanted to regulate these financial instruments, and that made some very powerful men angry. Born recalls, "They said I was pressing it. Well, I believed it. I thought that the country was in danger. I thought that the American public was going to suffer if we didn't do something."

She was publicly pilloried as being "difficult," "stubborn," and "strident."

Born says that she had to ignore those labels. "If you stick to your guns, we all know that a woman behaving the way a man would is described by a different adjective," she tells me. "But when it's important, it's important to do more to be heard." Now, a decade later, she can laugh about her own bad press, but she asks, "I mean, how many men are called *strident*?"

Still, Born was basically forced out of her job by then Federal Reserve Chairman Alan Greenspan and Treasury Secretary Robert Rubin.

SO WHAT DO YOU DO WHEN YOU'RE BEING IGNORED?

Sheila Bair insists, "Don't be embarrassed about sticking up for yourself and proposing good ideas. Try and carry the day at meetings, and if someone else tries to poach [your ideas], stand up for yourself and say, 'Well, that's exactly what I just said.' You can do that politely—you don't have to be confrontational."

Carol Bartz, however, is happy to be confrontational. When this happens to her, she tells me, "I say, 'I think I just said that about ten minutes ago.' I do that. Come on, they are not going to get away with that shit. I say, 'I said that ten minutes ago, what was it about the way I said that that didn't really work for you guys?' You have to do that. There's nothing wrong with that—it's a perfectly legitimate question."

Bartz points out that men will also use the passive-aggressive tactic of not responding at all. "You know, where they seem to agree but they really don't," she says. "I've always said, if you have an opinion, I don't care what it is, we have a starting point. Which means I can convince you differently and you can convince me differently. But if I don't know what you're thinking and then you leave and I think you think one thing and you never did, we will never get anything done."

Elizabeth Warren says what has worked best for her is "to let the men talk, but then to say, 'Yes, but let me ask that question again . . . maybe I didn't quite hear the answer, but let me push on that again,' because it means I'm listening, I'm treating this as a two-way conversation and I have noticed that you danced away from the central point. . . . For me that's always been the most effective."

But former GE CEO Jack Welch argues that women don't have to do anything to be heard: "When we're in a meeting and a woman speaks up—because they don't often speak up—when they do you can hear a pin drop."

I think he's probably right in situations where there's only one or two women: you stand out by virtue of being the only one of your kind. But more often than not, women have to try harder to be heard.

All the tools mentioned here add up to one piece of advice: be confident enough to raise your hand. Men just seem to have an easier time doing it, but making yourself visible is no less important for women. Bringing attention to yourself, your ideas, and your achievements means you'll be scrutinized. And if you fail, people will ask whether any woman can handle the job. But it's hard to get ahead if you're invisible.

Personally, I can use each one of these pieces of advice on the set of *Morning Joe*, and I work every day to keep them in mind.

CHAPTER 6

AT THE BARGAINING TABLE
Table Manners and Tactical Maneuvers

MY STORY, WITH SUZE ORMAN, CAROL BARTZ, LESLEY JANE SEYMOUR, KATE WHITE, ARIANNA HUFFINGTON, DONNY DEUTSCH, VALERIE JARRETT, TINA BROWN, HANNAH RILEY BOWLES, CAROL SMITH, NORA EPHRON, FRANK FLYNN, DONALD TRUMP, JACK WELCH, AND JOY BEHAR

NEGOTIATE LIKE A POWERFUL WOMAN

Personal-finance expert Suze Orman says the reason my attempts to get a raise failed is that I didn't know how to "negotiate like a powerful woman." I should have done my homework and come to the table armed with information and alternatives, not just a catalog of emotions and self-doubt. "The problem is that fear of failure comes when you haven't properly prepared for success," she says. "I am sure that you went in to negotiate your salary from a place of fear, and fear is one of the main internal obstacles to wealth."

What follows is a wealth of advice from a variety of women (and men) about what to do (and not do) when you're asking for a raise or negotiating a job offer.

KNOW YOUR CONTRIBUTIONS AND THEIR MARKET VALUE

In her book *Women & Money: Owning the Power to Control Your Destiny,* Suze Orman gives detailed advice to women on how to protect themselves financially and get the money they deserve. She orders women who want a raise to be prepared. First, document your achievements, and put together a list of all the ways you have met and exceeded expectations. Then, "Tell your boss you want to set up a meeting to discuss your compensation. Prior to that meeting, you are to give your boss a one-page outline of your achievements. Not ten pages—one page. The idea is that you are stating in clear terms what value you have brought to the company and why now is the time for the company to show that it values your effort."

The fact that you deserve a raise or haven't had one in years is not a persuasive argument. What makes a persuasive argument are solid facts and figures about what you've done and what other people, with the same skills and experience and accomplishments, are making for the same job.

Let me say it again: You are not prepared unless you know the market value of your contributions. I can't stress this enough. Why is it such a big secret? Seriously. What are you worth? What I've learned is, you should constantly be asking people about salary. Really wrap your arms around what work is worth what. The more you talk to people and the closer you get to them, the more they will tell you. Go ahead—ask. At this point I pretty much know what everybody is getting paid at

MSNBC, and I think that's part of my job, in terms of knowing my value.

For decades, companies have prohibited their employees from sharing information about their wages. In January 2009, Congress introduced the Paycheck Fairness Act, which was intended to ensure that women get paid as well as men for equal work. But the legislation, which would have made it easier for women to sue employers who pay them less than men and made it illegal for employers to retaliate against workers who shared information about wage practices, was defeated by the Senate in November 2010.

Even if you're prohibited from asking your colleagues directly about their own salaries, general information about salary ranges is widely available. This is the value of interviewing at other companies and maintaining contacts across your industry. I encourage people to talk—not just to other women in your field, who may be making less just like you, but to men as well. You can find out what people think the range is or what they think you should be making without directly asking about their salary or telling them yours. Over time, you really do learn the market rate for certain positions. I have a husband in my industry, which helps. I know what local anchors make compared with what network anchors make, what anchors make compared with what reporters make. Naturally every case is different, but you can get a sense of the range.

If you're in an industry that uses them, agents can be a great resource on the subject of fair market value. Because agents represent more than one person, they should be able to fill you in on what others make—or at least give you a ballpark. And if they're giving you bad information, they are not good agents. It's their job to be in the know. So utilize them wisely. Don't just wait for the phone to ring. Make a strategy, and then stick to it.

But it's also just kind of instinctive. I mean, seriously. I signed a contract that I intuitively knew was not right. I knew that I was worth more. But I let fear, and the potential of being disliked, supersede my instincts.

When I started at MSNBC again, as a freelancer, I knew what I signed up for. I had no complaints about that. And by the way, punching in at the same time and punching out at the same time every day—to me that was worth my making a lot less. That was fine. But when I started on *Morning Joe*, when I started to become part of a brand of two people, Joe and Mika, or when we became a team of Joe, Mika, and Willie, then we were a commodity. I knew what they were making, and yet I accepted less. I would love to believe that I'm alone in that stupidity. But I fear I'm one of many.

* * *

Our survey found that men are more likely than women to know what their peers are earning.

* * *

Researchers say part of the reason why women don't know what their peers are earning is social norms. They may not feel that discussing money is appropriate, because making a ton of money fulfills a masculine ideal, not a feminine one.

Despite the fact that we've been in the workforce for generations, the cultural ideal of women as caregivers hasn't shifted. Women are still expected to be more selfless than men, so even talking about money—let alone asking for it—makes us uncomfortable.

Carol Bartz says that while women will compare themselves with their colleagues, "the women don't always find out as easily what everybody else makes. The men seem to find out somehow. And I don't know why that is."

These days it's easier than ever to find out what people make. Employees share salary information on Web sites such as Vault.com and Glassdoor.com; sites like Payscale.com and Salary.com can give you an idea of salaries for comparative positions in your geographic area. But nothing beats talking with people.

More magazine editor-in-chief Lesley Jane Seymour says, "A big problem with women is that they go in not having done their homework; they don't know what everybody else is making . . . If you do your homework, then you walk in and you present your facts and you can say, 'Here's what other people in this company at the same level are paid. Let me show you all the facts and figures.'" Seymour doesn't think it's easy for anyone to ask for a raise, even men, because in that situation you feel like a child asking for their allowance. Everybody struggles. Again, "The key is to do your research. The most important thing that people don't realize, especially women, is you can't go in there expecting people to take care of you and that they're going to be fair. They're going to try to get the best deal they can."

WHEN YOU'RE ASKING FOR A RAISE, PICK YOUR MOMENT

Cosmopolitan's Kate White offers some advice about timing: "Often women wait to deal with their raise when it's announced to them, but by that time it's already etched into the budget. You need to go in a month or so before you know they're going to start giving the raises and just say, 'Look, I know you're probably planning the budget, and I'd just like an opportunity to tell you how much my job has expanded this year, and I hope my raise can reflect this.'"

AND THEN JUST DO IT

If you're prepared—you've documented your achievements and you know the fair market value of your work—it should be easier to take the emotion out of asking for a raise. It's no longer about you, it's about the facts in front of you.

* * *

Asked to describe how they felt when asking for a raise or promotion, men used words like "cool," "deserving," "confident."

* * *

Women used metaphors such as "like filing taxes," "like I was going to vomit."

* * *

One woman said, "I felt that the boss was a giant and I was a midget. I felt as if his/her eyes were burning a hole into my being as well as reading my mind."

* * *

The Huffington Post's Arianna Huffington urges women to be fearless: "Really, what's the worst that can happen? We are told no, and we're no worse off than we were before. Just look around and you'll see plenty of evidence that asking for what we want results not in the realization of our worst fears but in getting what we want."

Ultimately, as Donny Deutsch says, "You have to ask for it, and that's that."

Here's another thing to remember: when you realize that every raise you'll get in the future is a percentage of what you're already making, if you don't push to make more money right now, the cumulative effect a few years down the line will be enormous.

* * *

"You stand in front of that mirror and you practice until you are confident. You go in there and you be an actress."—CAROL BARTZ

* * *

Whether you're accepting an offer or asking for a raise, ask for more money with confidence. And if you don't have it, fake it. Carol Bartz tells me a story about a female friend of hers. "[She] was after a senior position in a company, and she knew she was a finalist and a guy was the other finalist. She was expecting a salary of $90,000 and maybe 2,000 shares of stock or something like that. She found out that this guy was asking $125,000 and 2,000 in stock. And she called me, and she said, 'What should I do?'"

Bartz instructed her friend to march in and tell them that she wanted $125,000 dollars and the stock too, but she balked. "She said, 'Oh, I can't do that. I couldn't keep a straight face.'"

Bartz tells me her friend honestly felt that she wouldn't have to tout her value, that it was obvious. But Bartz insisted: "I said, 'You stand in front of that mirror and you practice until you are confident. You go in there and you be an actress.'"

Bartz's friend got the job and the money.

I should add that acting should be a last resort. It's never worked for me (and in fact led to some pretty awkward moments with Phil Griffin). At some point in your life, you have got to know your value. It's your job to feel it and communicate it effectively. A strong sense of self-worth will serve you well in your relationship with your employer, and in any other relationship.

HOW NOT TO ASK

Many of us need to rethink the way we ask for promotions and raises, because when we do ask, often it ain't pretty. Just listen to the answers I hear when I ask, "Are there differences in the way men and women ask you for raises and promotions?"

* * *

" 'I know you're busy, I know you don't have time . . .' "—VALERIE JARRETT

* * *

Obama adviser Valerie Jarrett has been the boss in a variety of workplaces. When I ask whether she sees a difference in approach between men and women when asking for raises and promotions, she says, "Amazingly, men are almost detached from it emotionally. They're really comfortable . . . Women are much more timid and appreciative and polite. Men are very matter of fact, businesslike, unemotional. It isn't really personal."

"Women are emotional?" I ask.

"Emotional in the sense of apologetic . . . I remember one woman in particular who started with, "I know you're busy, I know you don't have time . . ."

"Basically saying, 'Don't give me the raise'?"

"She backed into it badly, is the way I would say it." Valerie tells me.

"Apologetic" and "tentative" are two adjectives I heard over and over. The editor-in-chief of *Newsweek* and *The Daily Beast*, Tina Brown says women often start to apologize with their body language before they even open their mouth. Then they'll begin by saying, "Well, you know, I've been here for a while and I've been thinking a lot about this . . . Men come in and they just say, 'Hey, I'm not doing this anymore unless I get X.' And you think, 'Of course, of course, of course,' you know, you must take care of Joe, Fred, whomever. But women don't do that. They just come in and they look sad . . . And we can't do that!"

* * *

"'I didn't really want to come to you with this . . .'"—CAROL BARTZ

* * *

I ask Yahoo CEO Carol Bartz, "Have you ever had a woman ask for a raise and apologize for imposing?"

"Oh, absolutely," she says. Bartz trots out a few she's heard: "'I didn't really want to come to you with this, but, gosh, do you think my bonus percentage could be higher?' And, 'Gee could you just think about it?' When they say, 'I don't know if you'll consider,' right away they are giving you an out. Of course I wouldn't consider, you just told me not to consider . . . when somebody gives you the reason you can say no, it just makes your job easier."

And men?

Men will say "'I believe I'm undervalued here,'" Bartz tells me. "And that's always code for 'I'm going someplace where they value me, and it's for these reasons.'"

"When men ask for raises there's always some cost," ad exec Donny Deutsch says. "It's always 'because I did this' and 'if I don't get the raise . . .' There's always [an imaginary] gun to the head, some gamesmanship. First of all, women don't ask as much. And when they do ask, it's not 'Give it to me or else.'"

When you combine my experience with what I heard from the bosses above, I have to say we women stink at this. Just look at our best opening lines:

- "I'm sorry."
- "I know you're busy."
- "I don't know if you have the time."
- "I don't know if you'll consider . . ."
- "I don't know if this is possible . . ."
- "I hate to do this."
- "I don't know if there's room for this in the budget."
- "I'm sorry if the timing is bad."

I think I've managed to use every one of those phrases in my attempts to get a raise. Of course, I used an additional strategy, too—what *More* editor Lesley Jane Seymour calls "playing the victim card." Seymour says women "present their personal challenges, saying things like, 'Well, I have this situation' or 'I have that burden' or 'My mother is ill and I have to support her' or whatever. Women present their cause, and you have to realize it's not a manager's job to support your causes, whatever they might be . . . The companies can't say, 'Oh, I feel sorry for you.'"

HOW TO ASK

Professor Hannah Riley Bowles has done research that supports the idea that playing the victim card is unlikely to work, because it's an explanation that's all about you; a more effective argument is one that taps into the organization's interests. You have to explain why a raise would make sense to the person you're talking with and to the company as a whole. She says the less effective route is "going in and laying down your credit card and saying, 'I can't buy the shoes I want to buy.'"

Bowles says the smarter approach if, for instance, my request for a raise had been denied but I still wanted MSNBC to cover my hair/makeup/wardrobe costs, might have been to say something like, "I think it makes sense for this job to have an expense account." I could have tried enlisting Phil's support in my efforts to project a professional image because my personal presentation has a direct impact on the show.

Bowles offers another tactic: "[One executive woman] told me she found out that a couple subordinates of hers were being paid more than she was. She tried going in and basically referring to it as an error that she knew the company would want to correct. Obviously the company is not going to want subordinates paid more than superiors, right?" Bowles's latest research shows that women are more successful when they explain the appropriateness of their request in a way that communicates their desire to maintain good relationships at work. "The trick is trying to do both of these things at the same time and in a way that feels authentic and fits within the norms of the company," she says.

Suze Orman says the way to get what you want is to offer your boss a choice. "You should never, ever, ever ask a yes or no question. If you ask for a ten percent raise and the boss says no, what are you going to say?" Instead, she suggests giving your boss two options: slightly more than what you want and then a lower number that you actually expect to get. "So you would say, 'I really think I deserve a ten percent or twelve percent raise. Which one would you like to give me?' At that point the boss really doesn't know what to say, because that's not a yes or no question, and the power has shifted into your court. It's very difficult for anyone to come back and say 'Neither.'"

Long-time *Elle* publisher Carol Smith tells me that the way men do it is to take the emotion out and simply say, "I've earned this. I'm coming in because here's what I've done over the last year, and now I've earned this raise." But she's always taken a softer approach: "I've often said that I don't want to be paid more, but I never want to be paid less. I want to be paid equal to the man sitting next to me who's bringing in the same amount of revenue."

Nora Ephron echoes those sentiments. "The words *favored nations*—that's an expression all women should know," she says. "In other words, you always want to be paid no less than what anyone else is being paid. If you're at all a wussy about valuing yourself, you can't be a wussy about the words *favored nations*. All you're asking for is what everyone else is making."

Valerie Jarrett uses the same favored-nations argument, but with a different delivery. "I don't like to negotiate salary at all, and one way I've compensated for that is by saying to someone, 'I expect that you'll be fair to me,' and then when they're not, I talk back. I say, 'I know you'll treat me fairly so you decide.' Then I come back and tell them they can do better."

Of course, saying "I expect you'll be fair to me" implies that both employer and employee share an understanding of what "fair" means. If you've done your homework, you know what both women *and* men with comparable experience and skill sets are making at your level.

ASKING FOR MORE

Kate White urges women to push the envelope. "You cannot be afraid to ask for more. But you have to do it in a way that is not emotional . . . What you really have to do is make it about what your value is," she says. "Stay very neutral and say, "I'm very happy to have the offer. It sounds like a great job. I was looking for $90,000 based on my experience and skills." They always, almost always, have more. As a boss I know that if you really want somebody, except in a recession where sometimes your hands are tied, you can go back and get more."

White says that after years of working in women's magazines and publishing articles about women's issues, she learned not to apologize and not to overexplain. But it takes practice. She says when you try to negotiate an offer, management might very well be shocked by your audacity. In which case, "You've got to learn to be very careful and keep it neutral and light, like a game," White tells me. You have to walk a line between being too deferential and too aggressive, but practice makes perfect.

"Every time you have one of those conversations, you get better at it. I had a situation once where I was using a lawyer, and they were giving the lawyer a terrible time. Basically they were indicating that they were getting frustrated with me because they felt I was asking for too much. I went in myself at that point and had a conversation, and in that conversation I realized okay, I've got to back off a little. I said some things like, 'I sense I've really frustrated the hell out of you. I'm sorry about that.'"

Is White really recommending that women apologize for putting a number on their worth? "I wasn't apologizing for what I was asking. I was apologizing that the lawyer's situation had frustrated them," she explains. "I corrected the situation in fifteen minutes and I remember the lawyer later said to me, 'You're better at this than you're giving yourself credit for.' I think that the more you do, the more you step back and learn from the previous experiences. I try to pay attention to body language, and of course to whether I get what I want in the end, so that the next time I can take all of that into consideration."

BE PERSISTENT

Stanford Professor Frank Flynn says that when women negotiate, they aren't as persistent as men are. "It's not that they don't ask, they don't ask ten times. And that's often the difference I see between women and men in business. Women assume no means no in a negotiation, and the negotiation is over." Flynn says men hear no as a signal "to take a different tack."

Suze Orman insists that if you're discussing a raise with your boss and you're not getting anywhere, "No matter how uncomfortable your boss tries to make you feel, I want you to stay right in your seat and keep the conversation going. If you know the company is on shaky financial ground, then of course you have to take that into consideration. But if the company is profitable and you are in fact a contributor to that profit, then you are not to walk out empty-handed." She suggests asking for another review in six months, and asking (and getting in writing) what raise to expect at that time. Meanwhile, ask for more vacation time or flexibility or whatever will be valuable to you. Orman says, "You must get something of value, for you are not on sale."

I can tell you from personal experience that all is not lost if you don't get what you deserve the first time around. Look at me: I had to go back a half dozen times! You may very well encounter resistance, even bullying, but there's much to be gained by holding your ground when you're presented with an offer that doesn't benefit you.

* * *

"Women throw around the emotional thing."
—Lesley Jane Seymour

* * *

More editor-in-chief Lesley Jane Seymour tells me a story about two female friends who recently got new jobs at the same company. They were negotiating with a senior woman at the firm. Seymour says, "When they got the job offer, they each said 'Let me have my lawyer look at this,' and they were told 'Oh, that would mean starting out on the wrong foot, let's not go down that road . . . so why don't you just sign right here.'" Seymour says she was appalled when her friends—two "very savvy women"—ended up signing without having their deals reviewed by an attorney.

"When I found out these two friends of mine did that, I said to them, 'Do you mean to tell me that you signed this thing without a lawyer looking at it?' I said, 'Do you think the woman who did this to you would ever sign her contract without a lawyer looking at it?' And the answer is no. . . . To me that was something that only a woman would do to a woman. Women know women respond to that. No woman would say that to a man, because a man sitting across the table would say, 'This has nothing to do with starting out on the wrong foot, this is business . . . I'm taking it to my lawyer,' and that would have been the end of the discussion."

Cosmopolitan's Kate White has a similar story about being pressured when accepting an offer. Years ago she was being pursued by *Working Woman* magazine. She went to talk to the owner, but at the time she wasn't really looking for a job. But the owner made her an offer almost immediately. White was caught off guard and wanted some time to think about making a move, but her prospective employer was giving her the full-court press. He wanted to make a fast hire, so he offered to sweeten the deal by giving her some equity in the company and kept calling her the next day.

She says she found herself dodging the owner's calls, still trying to weigh the offer's pros and cons. "Finally I called him back and said, 'Look, I don't think this is right for me,' but he really just pressured me. He was a fabulous sales guy on the phone. And I felt so guilty because I had stalled, and I couldn't really think of the right reason I couldn't go, so I buckled and said yes. . . . Later I wondered, 'How did I let myself get into this?' But I kept telling myself at least I've got the equity."

Looking back, White says, she just wasn't sufficiently comfortable in her own skin to say, "I don't care if he's pressuring me; I need to do what's right for me. I should have said to him, 'Look, you caught me off guard, offering me the job; I'm going to need a couple of days to really think this through.'"

IF THE ANSWER IS NO

Valerie Jarrett says her best advice comes from the lesson her parents taught her, "which is a hard lesson to learn, and that's not to be afraid of rejection. It's okay. Men aren't afraid of rejection. They're taught both personally and professionally that it's a part of the game. It's why men ask women on dates; they ask ten women out and if one says yes, that's great. Women would have a very hard time with nine rejections out of ten. You wear it on your sleeve. My parents always said to me, 'If you don't try, you're certainly not going to get what you want, so it's okay to fail and learn from your failure.' You should have enough self-confidence to pick yourself back up and get back on your feet. You have to reach high. I think women are willing to settle for a much smaller promotion. What's wrong with asking for the bigger promotion? You think people will think less of you if you do, but they actually think more of you."

Carol Smith was the first female ad salesperson for the *Wall Street Journal* at a time when women weren't doing that job. She says she must have some male gene in her makeup because she's "always been a very strong negotiator when it comes to salaries." But she knows plenty of brilliant women who have a hard time being paid their value and who have an equally tough time with rejection.

* * *

"She burst into tears . . . a hugely successful woman."—CAROL SMITH

* * *

Smith knows that emotions can handicap women at any age, and at any point in their career. She shares a story of a friend of hers who had recently taken on a great deal of additional work: "She had been doing basically three jobs in the last six months and had asked to be compensated. I knew what that job was worth because I'd had that job. So she was out to lunch with her boss and asked for the raise, and he said no. And she burst into tears." Smith points out that her friend wasn't a young woman, but an experienced executive. "I have known her for twenty years. She is brilliant, a hugely successful woman.

"She felt embarrassed and beaten down by this . . . she was going to walk away in tears, you know, and never go back." Smith told her friend that her boss's 'no' didn't have to be the end. Smith encouraged her to go back and work out a solution that both she and her employer could accept.

Smith tells me, "It helped me that I came out of sales. When you're in sales you have to learn to get rejected and constantly go back. When most of my non-sales female colleagues hear 'no,' they take it personally, and they think, 'Oh, I must not deserve this.' . . . When you're in sales, you've got to ask for that order over and over and over again, and you have to figure out a way to go ask for it a different way and say the same thing with a different ending."

BE READY TO WALK

Sometimes when the answer is no, you realize you're not going to get what you want now or possibly ever. That's when you realize it's time to get out. Tina Brown remembers the moment she realized it was time to leave Condé Nast. "I was editor at *The New Yorker*, my contract was coming up, and I wanted to play more of a role in the strategy of the magazine instead of just the editing. And the president of the company, Steve Florio, took me to lunch. I started to talk about how this was an issue in my contract. And he said to me, 'Where are you going to go? No one's going to give you a dress allowance like we do.'" Those words had her packing her bags.

Carol Bartz suggests that when push comes to shove, you better have your bags packed: "Now, what I will say to you is, you have to be ready to walk . . . I mean, when you are in a situation and you take a stand, you've got to be ready for the consequences. You know, when they look you in the eye and realize, 'This crazy bitch is going to leave.'"

And then there are times when the worst-case scenario becomes a reality, whether you like it or not. You ask, the answer is no, and you get fired! Real estate mogul Donald Trump says you can pester your boss to the point of no return. "I've had some very smart aggressive women working for me, and they are not shy about asking for things. That doesn't mean that they're going to get them, and in some instances they're so over the top in what they ask for that I fire them. Do you understand? I fire them. I say, 'Listen, I don't want to deal with this, you're fired . . . You work for a salary, you get a lot of money, and you're expected to make good deals.' . . . I have guys who make deals all day long, and if they came to me every time they made a deal, I'd go crazy."

If you deserve a raise, simply say it. But be prepared to leave and work somewhere else if management doesn't agree.

Former GE CEO Jack Welch says that successful salary negotiations depend on your level of confidence; if you know your skills are valuable, you know you'll find another, better job. "If you think it's easy for a guy to go in there and ask for money, I'm not sure it is. . . . I always felt if I didn't get what I liked, I was packing it in," he says. "I was ready to leave the day before I became chairman. I was always ready to pack it in, because I thought I could do well elsewhere."

Writer Nora Ephron suggests that quitting can be the best thing for your career: "You have to look at what men do. They quit, and they go somewhere else." That's how they improve their salaries quickly. But unless you like being unemployed, you need to be talking to other companies all the time and have an idea of where you're headed next. "The way to do it is you say, 'I need more money, I'm not being paid as much as so and so,' and you have to be prepared to leave. But you have to go sneak around and find somewhere to go. That's a very important thing, having somewhere to go when you quit," she says.

Comedian and talk show host Joy Behar will always have somewhere to go when she quits. She maintains her independence by keeping her comedy skills sharp. "One of the things that I've done in my career over the years is to have many irons in the fire," Behar tells me. "When I took *The View*, I did a lot of stand-up because nobody in television was going to control me. I could always make a living on the road." Now she has both *The View* and her own show, but she still does stand-up just to keep her options open.

Suze Orman points out that you can take the strongest negotiating stance of all when you have your financial safety net in place. "A woman can only be powerful when she doesn't need the money, otherwise she can't be powerful. You can't push somebody and say, 'This is what I want.' If you really need it and they let you go, what are you going to do?"

But Suze, how many women who ask for raises don't actually need the money? Orman responds, "What I'm saying is, the time to go in and ask for a raise with confidence is not when you have credit card debt, it's when you have an eight-month emergency fund. You also have to have a plan. Know your alternatives and come from a powerful place, not an insecure place. What gives you power? The answer is usually 'having money to fall back on.' You don't have to have a lot, just enough for you to know you'll be okay no matter what."

Orman recommends taking into account your entire financial picture before you start talking to your boss about money: "Not just what you're earning, but where is your money invested? How is it invested? Do you have all your wills and trusts? Do you have your insurance in place? Is everything together that creates a powerful woman? Because if it's not, you're walking into a negotiation powerless, and you will never be able to get the amount of money that you deserve because you're coming from a powerless place. It really is as simple as that."

She's right: the fact that I was in the red at the end of every month probably gave me an air of desperation. What I needed was an air of confidence.

When I tell Donny Deutsch that I had been an idiot about negotiating, he responds, "Well, then next time you're ready to do it, you talk to me first." The idea that Deutsch might be a more effective advocate for me than I am for myself speaks volumes about how powerless I was to get the money I deserved. And I think if most women really would look in the mirror, they'd see they aren't nearly as powerful as they should be either.

CHAPTER 7

ALLIES AND ENEMIES
A New Appreciation of Men in the Workplace, and a Warning About Women

MY STORY, WITH SHEILA BAIR, HANNAH RILEY BOWLES, MARIE C.
WILSON, SUSIE ESSMAN, TINA BROWN, ARIANNA HUFFINGTON,
AND BROOKSLEY BORN

JOE AND THE MONEY

When I got back to New York after the 2008 presidential primary season, I was demoralized and exhausted. After some soul-searching, I realized I could not go on being undervalued. I could not allow any managers, male or female, to exploit my insecurities. I could not back down any more. After years of letting myself be pushed around in an unforgiving profession, I was finally mature enough to know that when it came to being rewarded for my value, I was my own worst enemy.

Now was the time to make it right.

That is what brought me to the meeting with Joe at the

Rock Center Café. I felt Joe deserved an explanation. He had, after all, believed in me when no one else did. He had revitalized my career, and now I had to walk away.

I was transparent with Joe about the mistakes I had made. I also made it clear that whatever my own failings in getting my worth, the current pay structure between us was wrong. I had allowed it to persist for too long. I felt nauseated when I told him I would be leaving this job and a show that we both fought so hard to create.

"I've been working on something," he said. "Please wait another week. I have an idea. I see this as my business, and I see you as important to the success of that business. I need a chance to find a way to make you stay and feel whole. I won't ask for too much time. Just a few days."

A week later I went online to my checking account thinking I had run through my funds. I was expecting once again to be overdrawn and at least $2,000 in the red. Instead, I was shocked to find that I had more money in my bank account than I ever had had in my life.

I had not received the raise that I was looking for and was still not being paid what I deserved, but NBC had direct deposited a large amount of money into my account. Questions started racing through my mind.

Where did this money come from? (Had I won the lottery?) Would NBC give me a huge bonus without telling me first? (Not on your life.) Did the crack GE accountants accidentally add a few extra zeros to my paycheck? (A remote possibility.)

I soon learned, to my horror, that Joe had demanded that

MSNBC transfer his ratings bonuses to my account. These were payments Joe had negotiated in his contract. They were bonuses he received if *Morning Joe* ratings topped that of the Imus show, which we had replaced. While management never expected we could do that so quickly, Joe had banked on our success and soon tripled his salary.

So the money NBC had added to my account was actually subtracted from Joe's compensation.

I was furious. Raging. Humiliated. How could I accept this money? How weak and dependent would this make me look? How could NBC allow this?

Joe and I had ridiculous, loud arguments over whether I could accept his bonus pay. Although his public persona is quite different, when it comes to negotiations, Joe is introspective and calculating. Sensing that he was about to lose the cohost who would help him earn even more money down the line, Joe had sat down with his wife, Susan, to talk through their options for keeping me on *Morning Joe*. Soon they realized there was only one course of action. Joe would sign over parts of his ratings bonuses or lose me forever.

To Joe's agent and NBC, it seemed like a supremely generous gift to a cohost. To the Scarboroughs, it had less to do with charity than it did with the bottom line: I was a good investment.

While I understood their argument intellectually, I was still not emotionally prepared to accept a handout from a professional partner whom I considered to be my equal. So I did what I often do when confronted with a professional or personal crisis: I called my dad.

After I spent way too long explaining the situation, my father was ready to render a speedy verdict.

"Mika, it sounds like a shrewd business strategy on Joe's part. He is worth much more with you as his partner on the show than he is by himself. CEOs reward top performers with bonuses all the time. What makes this any different?"

That was a good question, and I had no good answer. My father was right. I would take the bonuses, not because I needed them but because I deserved them.

Joe's move had been generous, but as both my father and Joe pointed out, it was also a shrewd business move. We had a show that was on the upswing, whether MSNBC management could see it or not. He didn't want me to leave, he knew I was important to the show, and he knew that what was happening within the walls of 30 Rock was not right. He actually said that to the management: "You can be part of a *New York Times* article about our salary discrepancy, but I'm not." As is his habit, Joe Scarborough once again took matters into his own hands.

My frustration with my employer did not subside. I was emboldened by the fact that I knew I deserved the money. The investment that Joe made—and that's what it was, not a donation but an investment—made me realize something about myself that apparently I hadn't known even then. And that is, I was worth more. I mean absolutely, positively, unequivocally worth more. Why should I let Joe make up for MSNBC's shortfall? That was not going to continue; I was done. I finally knew my value and could not stay unless my employer recognized it, too. This problem was MSNBC's creation, but it was up to me to fix it.

I walked back into Phil's office, sat down, and spoke. My voice was low and sounded different, but it was me talking. Really talking. Not acting. Not venting. Not whining. Just talking in my own words: "You are a bad boyfriend. Do you know what that is, Phil?"

I didn't wait for a response.

"You take and take and take, but never give. Start giving," I said.

I went into great detail on the definition of a bad boyfriend. It was a little weird, and I probably wasn't saying just the right things, but it was calm and completely from the heart. Even better, I was ready to walk out the door with nothing and leave MSNBC for good. And the company knew it.

Phil actually took a moment, and then said, "You're right. We will fix this. I will fix this."

Time had also passed since our "crazy" talk, and we had had a chance to get to know each other, so he could truly find out that I was indeed crazy—but in a good way.

Within months, I had a new contract. It wasn't perfect. I am still paid considerably less than Joe, but at least I'm moving in the right direction. I got a good deal at a tough economic time for the network. They came through, but more important, I came through for myself. What Joe did, his conviction and follow-through, emboldened me. He gave me the confidence and drive to make MSNBC compensate me directly. The bottom line was, this time I really was ready to walk. You get paid your value when you're ready to walk. And by the way, if you're worth nothing, you'll be walking anyway. So you have to know your worth, *then* be ready to walk out the door.

THE VALUE OF STRATEGIC ALLIANCES

Still, I could not get over the fact that it took a man to turn the tide. I was angry, mostly at myself, that it had come to that. A man giving a woman money in the workplace just didn't feel right to me. Joe set me straight: "You are taking yourself way too seriously. This isn't about you. This is about me making more money. Because if you stay, our ratings will go up. And that will mean more money for my family. Stop thinking that I am being generous to you. This is really a selfish business decision about *me.*"

Joe had morphed from cohost to business partner.

As he fought to keep me on *Morning Joe*, he pored over my contract and salary and then guaranteed me that between TV, radio, and books, I would equal the salary I earned at CBS News. I was skeptical, but he laughed me off.

"You don't know your value!" he would say. "You will be laughing all the way to the bank."

By the end of the year, he had made good on all his guarantees and more. I got a book deal, a radio show, and other business opportunities. Looking back, it occurred to me that Joe knew my value even better than I did, and he became offended and aggressive when others did not.

While I greatly appreciate what Joe did for me, I wish I could have achieved the salary I deserved without having him step in like he did. But I realize after talking to many successful women that it's not unusual for them to succeed only after forging strategic alliances with men.

This experience has taught me the importance of having allies. Why not accept help from people who value you? Men do it all the time. And by allies, I don't mean agents. Agents were helpless to get me the money I deserved. The fact is, no one, *no one* can negotiate for you. I may use an agent to handle paperwork and money and details and mechanics, absolutely. But when it comes to speaking for me, I have to do that.

Several women I interviewed mentioned having mentors who offered valuable assistance in their careers. Sheila Bair speaks both of mentors and of other influential men who helped clear a path for her.

* * *

"Throughout my career, I've been mentored by men."—SHEILA BAIR

* * *

For seven years, Bair worked as counsel to Senate Majority Leader Robert Dole and credits him with paving the way for her. "He was a big supporter of women, and he had a lot of senior women on the staff," Bair says. "Women with real power, not just symbols; they were true advisers to him. Especially back when I was starting my career, there weren't that many women to mentor you, because there just weren't that many [to begin with]. Sandra Day O'Connor, Elizabeth

Dole. I can count prominent women on my fingers and toes, so we did rely on men . . . Throughout my career, I've been mentored by men."

Bair tells me that during the financial crisis, it was Federal Reserve Chairman Ben Bernanke who helped her get her message across: "He was the one who first started really listening, especially on some of the bailout issues . . . Of course, that helped because Ben had a lot of credibility with the guys."

But what Joe had done for me was more than endorse my ideas. I had started thinking of him as a business partner, someone whose help I could accept without giving up control. But he'd done more than even an ordinary business partner. He had actually used his own paycheck, in addition to his personal influence, to advance my interests.

People who study gender and negotiation would call him a sponsor: someone who is willing to use their own social capital to help pull another up the corporate ladder.

Harvard's Hannah Riley Bowles says, "We do need men to sponsor women very badly; they're in positions of power. When men in a position of power decide to clear that path for you—make sure you get the right exposure, make sure you get to the right meetings—that means a great deal. And there are not that many women to do that for you, frankly. A lot of the women at the top reach back, but there's just not enough of them."

Sponsorship is more than mentorship. A mentor will advise an employee, give him or her feedback, offer career strategy, and explain the company culture. Companies invest considerable resources in mentoring programs, but research shows that mentoring doesn't necessarily translate into better jobs for women. Women can be mentored so much that it wastes their time. Sponsors, on the other hand, will do more by using their connections and their influence to advocate for an employee. Catalyst's research finds that "high-potential women are overmentored and undersponsored relative to their male peers—and that they are not advancing in their organizations." Without sponsorship, women are not only less likely than men to move up, but they're also more hesitant to pursue top roles.

Lack of sponsorship, mentors, and networks: this was a recurring theme in almost all my conversations on the subject of women and compensation. Women's advocate Marie C. Wilson says women just don't have the same useful connections that men do, and the effects can be profound: "In the finance industry and some of the more masculine legal industries, women are not part of those networks that men are a part of, whether it's golf or the clubs that they take people to at night. . . . And who gets seen, who gets promoted, are people who are a part of those networks." She also says that we have to find ways to make men more comfortable with sponsoring the opposite sex. "If you are a man, taking on a young man as a sponsor is much easier than taking on a young woman because there is a certain kind of tension about that relationship, people look at it differently."

Like me, many of the highly successful women I interviewed had also received significant help from men in their industry. Susie Essman tells the story of trying to join the

Friars Club, a century-old private club for entertainment-industry types, notably comedians, that's really a tale about sponsorship. Traditionally all male, the Friars Club didn't allow women members until 1988, and women weren't invited to their famed Celebrity Roasts. Essman says, "When they first asked me to do roasts, they didn't allow women to even sit on the dais . . . [the men's jokes] were all filthy, dirty, blue blue blue, and they didn't think our delicate ears could handle it. So when I first had to do a roast, I had to prove that I could be as dirty as them and yet not be vulgar. I had to keep that balance." Naturally, Essman proved herself, managing to be both feminine and filthy dirty, and also stay on point and deliver a punch line.

Years later, "There was a roast that Comedy Central was recording for Jerry Stiller," Essman says. "The Friars Club had put my name in because I had proven myself with all these old guys—Alan King and all these great old comics—who did not think women were funny at all. Comedy Central turned me down. They didn't want me on, and I do believe it was because I was a woman of a certain age and they wanted guys that were in their early twenties. The Friars Club, to their credit, fought for me to be on because I had proven myself over and over again. They put me on the show and I killed, and Larry David saw me on that show and called me up and gave me the part in *Curb*."

As Essman points out, "In show business, it takes one person to say, 'you know what, you're really good.'" It took Larry David, creator of HBO's *Curb Your Enthusiasm*, "who was a very powerful person in the comedy world, to say, 'I think this person is really talented and I'm going to give her a part on my show.'"

When I ask Essman whether she thinks a woman would have been able to do the same for her, she tells me, "I do think there are women in the business who would have been able to do that for me; there have been powerful women in the business. I don't think there are many. People say comedy is a man's world, but the world is a man's world."

Clearly, the more people you know—the more people who are willing to support your efforts—the more likely you are to succeed, and the more likely you are to be paid well. Research has shown that success really does depend on who you know. A study published in *Administrative Science Quarterly* in 2000 looked at the effects of different personal attributes on compensation and found that in terms of salary, candidates who knew just one person in the organization negotiated salaries that were 4.7 percent higher than those without social ties.

Professor Hannah Riley Bowles points out, "In general, we could certainly say, the better you know people, the more information they're likely to share, the more helpful they're likely to be to you. They can vouch for you, they can help you negotiate, they can lend social capital. They can say, 'This person is really . . . ,' they can present you in a very favorable light. There are a variety of things they can do in terms of quality of information that you get, the way you present yourself, knowing whom to talk to, knowing *how* to present yourself. You have to be authentic to yourself, but you also have to negotiate the way that fits the norms of the organization."

The Daily Beast's Tina Brown notes a difference in the quality of men's networks and women's networks. She points out that women just don't have the long history in the workplace that amounts to a female-networking tradition. "I think that networking background for women is just not there. When men get fired from these jobs, these big jobs, they have other men who step forward to look after them and get them jobs as presidents of this, or think tanks, or some big nonprofit. I mean, you see men being taken care of when they're fired. When I see women getting fired, there's no cushion of networking waiting to deploy them into other jobs. I just don't see it. I see men all the time being fired from their jobs and being looked after by their networks. . . . Women just don't have the deep bench of network."

But as I listen to women's stories and tell my own, I wonder whether part of the reason that women's networks aren't as powerful is because women aren't trying very hard to support one another.

SISTERHOOD IS POWERFUL . . . ISN'T IT?

Many of my interviewees cite evidence that other women not only weren't there to lend a hand, but they were actively undermining their efforts to get ahead.

Are women harder on other women? It may just be that women managers are more effective with women because they know which buttons to push. Who better to exploit the weaknesses that hold women back than a woman? I'm reminded of Lesley Jane Seymour's story about the female manager who discouraged her friends from having their contracts reviewed by a lawyer.

Women need to learn how to respond to these tactics.

What follows is an example of what I've done, and it is a textbook case of what *not* to do. I repeat: women managers know all too well what strategies to use to keep us cheap.

THE MIDDLE MANAGER, A WOMAN, TELLS ME NOT TO GET THAT RAISE

Ironically, the only time I was brought to tears at MSNBC over my pay problems was in a conversation with a middle manager who happened to be a woman.

She called a meeting to discuss my salary dispute, and the mood quickly turned sour. This manager insisted that I back off my request for a pay raise and told me that my demands were badly timed. Then she really dug in: "Mika, people won't like you. You are going to get a bad reputation. You need to stop." This woman knew Joe's salary was fourteen times mine—a huge disparity. But she was skilled at getting me to change my focus.

She kept me in her office for thirty minutes, arguing that I would ruin my reputation and that my request for more equitable pay would cost me in popularity. She said this with a clear warning in her voice, even a threat. "People will see you as a problem," she said. She told me I should be focused less on earning my value and more on winning MSNBC's Miss Congeniality prize. Was she serious? Sadly, she was—and her strategy worked.

Looking back on that day three years later, I cannot believe how naïve I was. I was shocked to tears that a woman would push another woman to accept such a degrading situation. I am even more pained to admit that I actually started worrying about whether my coworkers would stop liking me if I pressed for the raise that I so clearly deserved. It was obvious to this female manager that while I was used to being liked in newsrooms, I had no idea what it was like to be paid a salary that matched my worth. So she did what any effective manager would do. She went in for the kill.

When it comes to gender politics, how women treat other women in the workplace is a sensitive and fraught topic. I've had wonderful female bosses and not-so-wonderful ones. I've spoken with women who loved their female bosses and those who described relationships with female bosses that were complicated by generational experience and by differences in life choices. And several times since *Morning Joe* began, a female manager played into my feminine fears and tendencies with the sole intent of holding me back. The Paris Hilton incident, the red hair clip reprimand, this dressing down when I asked for a raise: the most painful and least constructive confrontations I've had in my career have been with

152

women. Ladies, we should be ashamed of ourselves. In the highest levels of business, we are our own worst enemies. Before we can fix this problem, we first have to admit to it.

Arianna Huffington believes it's vitally important for women to be truly supportive of one another: "Indeed, I talk about building our 'fearlessness tribe,' surrounding ourselves with women—and men, of course!—who will always be in our corner, always there for us, whether we succeed or fail.

"It's very important for older women, those who have gone before, to give a hand up and to mentor younger women in a consistent, sustained way—which is ultimately sponsoring them. Finding a sponsor is very similar to asking for a raise: if you don't ask for help, no one is going to just give it to you.

"I think women need to do what men have always done: reach out and connect. In some ways, social media have made this easier. And there are more and more conferences for women, places to meet and learn from women who have done the things you are interested in doing." Huffington recently cohosted the WIE [Women: Inspiration & Enterprise] Symposium, with Sarah Brown and Donna Karan, bringing together women from all walks of life for inspiration and empowerment, and to take action for the betterment of all women.

* * *

Our survey found more than half of all men and women agree that women are harder on

other women in the workplace than they are on men.

* * *

I ask former CFTC chairman Brooksley Born about the impediments women still face, and how she thinks we could overcome them. She, too, argues that women should be helping one another out. "It's really important for women to try to work together to change things in the workplace, to open opportunities, and I think it needs to be talked about. I think women need to support each other and cooperate with one another. They need to seek out male allies in the workplace, and they need to work as a group to change workplace policies to make them more amenable for women to be treated equally."

I ask her, "Do you think that women aren't helping other women? Or not helping them as much as they should?"

"Well, I think there's a need for more. I do think there's a lot of mutual support—not universal, obviously. But when there was a lot of discrimination, in the 1970s for example, it was easier to get people activated. Women consciously got together to network and work together and support each other in many big cities around the country. And I don't know the extent to which that is going on with the younger age groups today. Luckily there are a lot more venues where they can do it. There are wonderful Women's Bar Associations, and associations of women journalists, and associations that aren't gender specific, for people who are like-minded to get together and work on these issues."

Born's last piece of advice for women coming up in the ranks today is exactly that—stick together and help each other. She encourages younger women "to make sure they are continuing to work together for more equal treatment and economic opportunities."

CHAPTER 8

MOTHERHOOD
The Game Changer

MY STORY, WITH SHEILA BAIR, SENATOR CLAIRE MCCASKILL, DONALD TRUMP, LESLEY JANE SEYMOUR, SHERYL SANDBERG, NORAH O'DONNELL, CAROL SMITH, BROOKSLEY BORN, VALERIE JARRETT, TINA BROWN, CAROL BARTZ, KATE WHITE, AND MARIE C. WILSON

IOWA AND BEYOND

Throughout my weeks on the road covering the primaries in 2008, I never mentioned my two girls. A woman talking about her family seemed out of place at work. Joe freely talked to his wife and children on the phone and talked about flying them to our various locations as we traveled state to state. But I never felt that I could. I suspected the men I worked for might think less of me if I did. This was in my mind, not theirs.

I would call my family and tell them how much I missed them, and at times I deeply yearned for their presence. But you never saw it on my face when I was working. After all those years in the business, I still didn't feel comfortable "raising issues" about needing to be with my family. I suffered alone, as did they. I wish I had felt more comfortable, and I wish I could have afforded to bring them along and expose them to the story. Joe's ability to do that made me envious.

When it comes to wages and advancement, the gender gap is widest for working mothers. Research shows that women's earnings go down for each child they have. Part of the gap in wages and advancement for mothers is because they take time out of the workforce or cut back on hours. But studies also indicate that even if they don't cut back, mothers still earn less.

In a study titled "Getting a Job: Is There a Motherhood Penalty?" researchers Shelley Correll, Stephen Benard, and In Paik at Cornell University asked participants to evaluate resumes for two equally qualified job candidates: one was a mother, the other was not. Mothers were consistently ranked as less competent and less committed than non-moms. They were also offered, on average, $11,000 a year less pay.

Representative Carolyn B. Maloney, Democrat of New York and the chairwoman of the Joint Economic Committee, recently commissioned a report based on an analysis of census data. "When working women have kids, they know it will change their lives, but they are stunned at how much it changes their paycheck," Maloney said. The data shows that across the workforce, the pay gap is slightly wider for managers who have children. Managers who are mothers typically earn seventy-nine cents of every dollar paid to managers who are fathers, and that gap has stayed the same for at least a decade. Could the difference be explained by discrimination?

Most mothers I spoke to were well aware of the way they are perceived. Sheila Bair is the mother of two children. "Talking about family can be viewed negatively by men, like you're more focused on that than your work. Or that those are soft issues and you're not serious," she tells me. "I always come to work with a purpose, but I do think I generally do not talk a lot about my family in front of my male colleagues unless they initiate it. But some men love talking about their kids."

"Men look great when they're talking about their families," I say.

Bair agrees. "That's right, but women can be perceived as being diverted from our careers if we talk about our families."

* * *

"I watched one focus group on me, and they had a woman call me Cruella de Vil."
—CLAIRE MCCASKILL

* * *

Missouri senator Claire McCaskill's career illustrates the mine-laden path to success that women must follow. McCaskill has spent the past three decades running for political office. Her first bid was for the job of Kansas City prosecutor, which she describes as "a very male-dominated world." At the time, McCaskill had just given birth. "I had just had my third child," she says, "and all my children were very young, and the traditional thing is to show your children to humanize you and so forth. When I ran for prosecutor, there was never a mention of my children, and I did that because

I worried first that people would think, 'She has young children, she shouldn't have that job' . . . I was worried that people would think I wasn't tough enough to do the job, that I somehow wouldn't be able to come down hard on violent criminals.

"There had never been a woman elected to that office, and so I was trying to convince people. My commercials were all about the fact that the police had endorsed me and never mentioned the fact that I had three small children." McCaskill won the election.

Years later, McCaskill ran for governor, but she was defeated. During the campaign her emphasis was to show people "that I was smart and that I was confident, that I could do this job." After McCaskill lost, a journalist told her, "[she] couldn't decide whether I was more the model of the obnoxious teacher's pet or the really obnoxious contestant on *Jeopardy*. I had all the answers, but the feedback we seemed to get from the voters was that tough was not the problem, competence was no longer a problem, it was whether or not they wanted to spend any time with me. You know—whether there was that likeability. It was just incredibly shocking to me that after spending my entire career worrying about showing everyone that I was up to the job . . . now all of a sudden I had to make sure they knew that I truly like to cook and I truly adore and worship my children."

Fast-forward a few more years. McCaskill ran for the Senate, and she once again struggled for that balance, making midcourse corrections. "When I was running, I watched one focus group on me, and one woman called me Cruella de Vil.

So that's when I realized people need to understand that I've got a family, and I've got the same fears and hopes and dreams for my kids that they have. And so at that point in the Senate campaign, my daughter was in one of the commercials— my daughter and my mom.

"How do you walk the line between the b-word and ambition? It's a very narrow tightrope at times, and how you walk that tightrope is a challenge in and of itself," McCaskill tells me.

* * *

"She's not giving me one hundred percent; she's giving me eighty-four percent, and sixteen percent is going towards taking care of children."
—Donald Trump

* * *

The real estate mogul and television personality Donald Trump hires a lot of women. I ask him, "So are we at the point where women employees who are mothers aren't as valuable, because we have kids and we balance other things? Or does having children actually increase our value?"

"I think the most important thing is the children, and frankly [caring for them means taking] time away, and an employer could say she's not giving me one hundred percent, she's giving me eighty-four percent, and sixteen percent is going towards taking care of children. So maybe you can also understand the employer's point of view."

"From my point of view," I tell Trump, "I give two hundred

percent, and then I give another sixty percent to my kids at home every day."

Trump replies, "There is a mathematical equation to it. No matter how much time you give, there are men who give one hundred percent of one hundred percent. You give one hundred percent of seventy-five percent. You can understand the employer's perspective."

I tell him that is a cruel bottom line. "It is," he responds, "except you have the advantage of having kids. That's also the bottom line, and that's more important than the other twenty-five percent."

More magazine's Lesley Jane Seymour agrees that some women don't pull their equal weight at work. "There are people who can't do both," she says. "I've seen that on staff, people who just can't manage to do both, and you know, they're never here, they're out, or they're making excuses."

Seymour believes those examples reinforce the stereotype. "[Employers] have one bad employee who falls apart when they are trying to handle a family, so they assume no one can do it. And they don't know about all the other incredible women who you don't even know have children, because they manage it so well."

Facebook COO Sheryl Sandberg says she sees women struggling to balance family and work even *before* they have children. "It's very hard to watch," she tells me. "I've hired all these men and women, and then eight years later the men are largely ahead of the women. And the women were just as talented." She notices that it isn't necessarily that women aren't raising their hands and asking for promotions or new opportunities in general; it's that they're not pushing forward specifically during their child-bearing years.

"The pattern is the following: a woman starts thinking about having a kid. Now maybe she's just thinking about it right as she gets engaged, maybe she starts thinking about it right as they start trying, but even if they're trying to get pregnant that minute, it's nine months to have the baby, three months of maternity leave, three months to catch your breath, that's already a year and a half. More likely they start thinking about this a year and a half before that, even two or three years, and at the moment they start making room for a kid, they stop looking for new opportunities. They think, 'Oh my god, I want to have a child, there's no way I can fit anything more.' So the men around them are busy—solving problems, looking for new opportunities, saying, 'I want the promotion, I want the transfer, I want the raise, I want the new job'—and the women start leaning backward." Sandberg argues that by the time women turn their full attention back to work, they've been passed over.

"So what's the solution?" I ask. "Don't have kids?"

Sandberg replies, "Keep your foot on the gas. My advice is, when you have a child you'll want to slow down, but don't slow down in advance of the child."

There's so much anecdotal evidence that having children impairs your ability to do well at work, but I sincerely believe that having children has made me a more valuable employee. The fact is, women like me overcompensate at work, to prove that having kids does not make us less effective. But we demand less in return for being so lucky to have kids and a job, as if someone gave us a gift when they doubled our workload and made sleep a thing of the past. This is something I have done throughout my career. I think the problem is that women buy into the idea that they can't contribute significantly both at work and at home, and as a consequence, they undervalue themselves.

* * *

"It's a common problem that mothers underestimate their worth and their value."
—NORAH O'DONNELL

* * *

Chief Washington correspondent for MSNBC Norah O'Donnell, a colleague and a good friend, tells me, "I guess the truly honest answer is that I probably would ask for more if I did not have kids, and that's a tough thing to say . . . I'm worried that I'll look like an ungrateful employee, that I'll seem ungrateful for the great job that I have.

"I think that it's a common problem that mothers underestimate their worth and their value. Mothers ask for less, demand less from their employers, because they already think that they are struggling with this balance of work and family . . . that guilt can then inhibit them from asking for more, because any free moment that they may have at work gives them an opportunity to make a doctor's appointment or a dentist's appointment or to order diapers online—but that is a false sense of guilt.

"I know that I'm there at work just as much as others, I work just as many long hours," O'Donnell continues. "I'm there before most people stroll into work, and I stay later. Mothers work hard and sometimes doubly hard, and are even more productive in some ways because they know they have only so much time to do that."

The truth is, in many cases having children adds to our value. We may not be more organized, but we use time far more wisely. We have babies to protect, so our decision-making skills revolve around real-life issues. We develop another dimension to our lives that make O'Donnell and me better reporters and storytellers. But with that also comes guilt. And it cuts both ways. We feel guilty that we can't give our kids more time—that goes without saying—but I believe working mothers also feel guilty about having great jobs. We feel that we're so blessed to have it all, and that feeling of luck undermines our ability to negotiate effectively, and gives managers the sense that we can be taken advantage of. We tend to work harder to prove that our kids won't be an impediment to our productivity. Take what the amazingly honest Carol Smith told me, which says it all:

* * *

"I love hiring women [for] four days a week because they actually will produce at least five days' worth of work for four days' worth of pay."
—CAROL SMITH

* * *

Former *Elle* publisher Carol Smith sees mothers undercutting their value. "I will say, as a person who has hired a lot of women who want to continue to work but also have their family, this whole idea of job shares and part time . . . they will do anything to have a four day week. Anything. They will work in the bathroom. They will work twenty-four hours during the four days they work to be able to get that fifth day at home.

"The women who are striving to work part time, whether it's three or four days a week, will sacrifice everything. And let's start with money. So if they're working four days a week, they don't say, 'I now want eighty percent.' They will accept sixty percent of their salary to be able to say, 'I can be at home with my family, and I can still keep my career.' They are so grateful for anything that they devalue their worth.

"I'll tell you something," Smith continues. "I once said, 'I love hiring women four days a week because they actually will produce at least five days' worth of work for four days' worth of pay.' And I have done that. I used to say four days was so much better than three. Three becomes a part-time job. Four is a full-time job done in four days!"

During our conversation, Smith becomes aware of exactly what she was admitting to. "It's only now that I'm sitting here and talking to you that I realize the implications," she says. "I will say, in the end, that however grateful we are for the work, going in there we women have to value ourselves higher."

* * *

Our survey found that the majority of both men and women feel that parenting skills should be valued in the workplace.

* * *

Nearly half of men and women felt parents should be rewarded for the skills they bring to the workplace (for example, with higher salaries or promotions).

* * *

Former CFTC Chairman Brooksley Born agrees that being a mother made her more efficient at work because she used her time more wisely and because working part-time kept her mind fresh: "I think that I certainly changed from being an employee without any responsibilities for children, who had the luxury of not being terribly efficient, to a mother who knew that every minute counted and I darn well better be concentrating. I think I became much more efficient, and it's helped me ever since."

Did Born overcompensate and work harder than she did as a full-time employee? "I don't think that [as a part-time worker I was contributing] one hundred percent," she says, "but I do think that I was doing more than fifty percent of my full-time work." Born does feel, however, that being a mother helped her be more productive. "I, myself, felt that working three days a week, I could contribute something more in three days than I could when I was working five and a-half or six days a week. Partly because I had a lot more stamina, partly because when I was in the office, I wasn't making personal phone calls or going out to lunch, or you know, any of the frills. I was really working. I also found that there was an advantage, to me at least, when solving complex strategy issues or complex legal questions, in getting away from the office, being with the children. I would work Mondays, Wednesdays, and Fridays, and so I had days off in between days of work. I would often come back to the office, and somehow or other my subconscious had gone a long way toward solving the problems. The most difficult strategy problems had been worked out while I was at the playground."

Valerie Jarrett agrees that being a mother taught her new skills. "Having children teaches you a certain conscientiousness and discipline and responsibility," she says. "I think what women have to do, that we don't often do, is recognize those broader life experiences add value, they don't subtract."

Did the fact that she was a single mom, trying to balance everything, affect her perception of herself and what she had to offer?

Jarrett answers, "Yes, very much so. Part of what gave me the strength to leave [an early job at a] law firm, quite frankly, was that I was not doing a very good job because I had no passion for what I was doing. I wanted my daughter to be proud of me, and I thought if I stayed on that track she wouldn't be. It wasn't just knowing that she was solely relying on me financially; she was solely relying on me as a parent. I remember looking at her and saying, 'You're all I have, and I've got to really do right by you.' So I think my daughter made me more ambitious and much more able to push myself, because I was pushing myself for her."

The Daily Beast cofounder Tina Brown agrees that women will handicap themselves by always taking family into consideration. "There's no doubt having children makes you do a kind of instant review of any problem that comes up, or any challenge or any opportunity with regard to the children," she says. "Immediately you think, 'Will this job mean that I have to travel more? I can't.' 'Will this job mean I have to work so late at night that I miss evening dinner with the kids? No, I can't.' You're tortured about how you're going to confront it. And to be honest, a lot of men, most men I think, even now, won't even [take the family picture] into the consideration of their job. They'll simply say, 'That's a great opportunity. Yes!'"

Brown and I also talk about the fact that women don't feel they can put family concerns on the table without immediately losing value. Especially at the executive level, we "immediately downgrade ourselves" if we raise those issues at work.

And as a result, we're less likely to take the time we need to recover physically from having a child. Brown remembers, "I had just given birth to my second child, my daughter, Isabel, in 1990. It was exactly that time that Condé Nast decided they were going to launch *Vanity Fair* in the U.K., which meant, I realized, that I was going to have to go to London." She was nursing at the time, so did she take the baby with her? Leave her home? She says she was also "enormously overweight. I had just had a child, I did not want to be starting on the promotion circuit having just had a child. I did not want to be posing for glamour shots instead of being at home quietly." Ultimately Brown decided she couldn't say no, and she couldn't take the baby on this incredibly demanding trip, so she went alone, and "was secretly distraught the whole time."

Brown didn't feel that she could tell her bosses that she needed to accommodate her postpregnancy body. "I knew that that date was going to collide but I didn't have the confidence to say, 'I will do this better in September, not in March, when my body's ready.' It would not have occurred to me to bring up that question early in the planning. And I just don't know if anyone would have heard me anyway," she says.

Brown's story resonated deeply with me, because I rushed back to work after my second child, and I should not have. One day I had a horrific accident with her. Working overnights and running on two hours' sleep, I had her in my arms when I fell down a flight of stairs, and she broke her thigh bone. I lived through hell knowing that my baby suffered so much pain because I wasn't managing my time and my sleep well. The fact is we've got to listen to our bodies and have the confidence to say, "You know what? I'll be there when I'm ready."

That said, how many companies are really willing to wait? For many women, saying "I'll be there when I'm ready" is the same as saying "I quit." Companies don't always have the money or patience to accommodate us, and we know that.

We can only control what we control, but one choice we can make is whether or not we work for family-friendly companies.

MSNBC's Norah O'Donnell notes that, "If you work for a good company, they're usually pretty understanding about it . . . [it's possible to find] male and female bosses who completely understand and are completely willing to work with you."

O'Donnell says that when she first started working in the Washington, D.C., bureau she was working seven days a week, filling in for whoever couldn't show up. "I was taking everybody's shift . . . anything to get on the air because I was a network correspondent at twenty-five, and I was lucky to be there. After a year or so I asked if I could have one day off. It was a weekend day, and I just wanted to get things done. I was told by the deputy bureau chief at that time, who was a woman, an unmarried woman without children, that if I ever asked for a day off again, I probably wouldn't get these assignments. What's fascinating is that it wasn't from a male boss. That was from a female boss, who I believe had been forced in a different era to make those concessions in order to get into a position of power, and she was just passing what she'd learned on to younger women."

O'Donnell also tells the story of how she felt tremendous guilt when she got pregnant with her third child, Riley, four and a half months after giving birth to twins, Henry and

Grace. O'Donnell's babies were born a decade after mine, yet we felt the same stress about telling our bosses the news. We both worried it would diminish our value or even disappoint our bosses. In both cases we were wrong.

* * *

"I was embarrassed to tell my boss, Tim Russert, that I was pregnant again."—Norah O'Donnell

* * *

"I was this hard-charging correspondent who's been all around the world," O'Donnell tells me, "who is always gone on call 24/7 and gung ho." In her mid-thirties, she decided she wanted to have kids, so she took a new position as chief Washington correspondent. It was as demanding a job as any other, but it involved less travel. She soon gave birth to twins and felt that she was just getting her momentum back at work when she found out she was pregnant again. She was so embarrassed to tell her boss, NBC News' Washington bureau chief Tim Russert, that she put it off until there was no way to hide the evidence.

When O'Donnell finally did break the news, she realized she was lucky to be working for someone who valued family, and who also valued her as an employee. "I was so silly to have been embarrassed to tell him, because Tim was more than thrilled," she says. "He was so excited, in fact, that he suggested the name Riley, which is what I ended up naming my daughter."

I had a similar experience years ago, when I discovered I was pregnant with my first child, Emilie. I pained over how to tell my news director at WFSB Channel 3 in Hartford, Connecticut. But like Tim Russert, my boss, Mark Effron, was ecstatic for me, and even suggested my pregnancy would be great for ratings. My daughter was due in January, but he joked, "Any way you could hold out till the May ratings book?"

Obama adviser Valerie Jarrett tells a story about the moment she realized she was working for the right boss. She was working for Chicago Mayor Richard Daley as the Commissioner of Planning and Development. She and Susan Sher, who was the corporation counsel, had just taken their jobs and were in one of their first meetings with the mayor. "I don't even know what we were talking about," Jarrett says, "but Susan and I were sitting across from each other, and the Mayor was at the head of the table. He could be a little intimidating. We keep looking at our watches, then looking at him, and he's talking and not paying much attention. Suddenly it dawns on him that we're not really 'in' the meeting—we're somewhere else. He pauses and says, 'What's going on? Clearly you guys have somewhere else you'd rather be, what's going on?' And in a moment of truth, Susan and I look at each other and make eye contact. I said to him, 'The Halloween parade starts in twenty minutes. Our kids are in the same class, and we've never missed a Halloween parade.' He pauses and says, 'Then why are you still sitting here?' It was like the weight of the world was lifted from our shoulders.

We go racing down Lakeshore Drive and we get to our children's school literally as these two little darlings are coming out of school in their costumes, and of course the first thing our kids do is look for us. I can't tell you how many times we've said to each other, 'What were we doing sitting there when all we had to do was ask?'"

Jarrett says part of the life lesson there is you've got to stick up for what you need and what's important to you: "If he had said, 'Well, I'm sorry but I need you to stay here,' then we were working for the wrong person," she tells me. "You shouldn't be afraid to find that out. The First Lady often tells the story about taking Sasha to a job interview because she couldn't find a babysitter, and she learned a lot about Mike Riordan, her boss, because it was fine with him. If it hadn't been fine with him . . . isn't it good to know that early?"

Those experiences have taught Jarrett to be a better boss: "I think as a manager I try to encourage women and men to feel empowered to ask for what they need. Everybody here has children and I'm always saying to them, 'Don't miss the Halloween parade.'" She says hard-working employees who are able to take a few hours off for personal issues are going to come back feeling terrific about their jobs, and they're going to continue giving their all.

Yahoo CEO Carol Bartz echoes those sentiments. "One of the things I say to people who work for me is, 'Your child only has one Christmas pageant, only has one concert, and there will be a staff meeting until the end of eternity, so you know, don't miss that stuff.'"

Cosmopolitan's Kate White tells the story of leaving her job when she realized she was working for the wrong boss. She was in the number-two position at *Mademoiselle* when she had her first child. Her boss, a woman without kids, called her into her office a week after White had returned from maternity leave and told her she didn't want her leaving at five o'clock every day. White didn't feel comfortable pointing out that the boss herself left at 5:30 every day, and that White was putting in extra hours every day after the baby went to sleep. At that moment, she says, "I stepped back and thought, 'What's going to give me more control?' I realized being an editor-in-chief would do that. Working at a different type of magazines such as a parenting magazine, would do that. When I heard about the job at *Child* opening up, I figured they don't want a bad mommy in that job. When I got to the third interview and they said, 'Do you have any other questions?' I leaned forward and I said, 'I'd just like to conclude by saying how much I'd love this job and I think I would be terrific at it, blah blah blah.' The publisher, who was a woman, later said that she loved that I asked for the job. I remember saying to my son Hunter later—even though he was a baby—lying on the bed with him, saying, 'You helped Mommy get a great job because you made me ferocious.'"

She adds, "I have to say, Mika, I think I did gravitate toward bosses who one, liked to give a long leash to their editors-in-chief, and two, understood being a working parent. So it was a combination. I was also lucky enough to be in a field where there's a lot of flexibility."

MARRY THE RIGHT GUY

In addition to keeping your foot on the gas and doing what you can to work for the right people, another key factor my interviewees acknowledged was getting help at home. Facebook COO Sheryl Sandberg says, "I think if we got to parity in the home, we'd get to parity in the workforce really quickly." When she's asked what the most important thing to do to get your career right is, she says, "Marry the right guy . . . the data is very clear that if a man and woman work full time, the woman does twice as much housework and 3.5 times the amount of child care. So she drops out because she's got two jobs. He's got one job, and he stays in his. So more important than any career decision you make, I think, is who you marry."

There's been a lot of discussion in the press recent years about the term "opt-out revolution." Are women just tired of being on the fast track? Do those who have the luxury of not working do so because they're just less ambitious? Or is it that working two jobs (the one you do at work and the other at home) really just break them? Women's advocate Marie C. Wilson says, "Women who are coming up [the leadership] pipeline have to make really tough decisions about children and work, because as you and I know, those jobs are 24/7, so you really have to decide, is that the way you want to live? Sometimes women don't want to make those choices. I used to not believe this, but I think increasingly women are saying, 'Why would I want to live like that?' And more men are too, as a matter of fact."

Wilson believes that the problem is the sociocultural ideal of women in America has never changed. While many women work as executives, society still thinks of them as primarily wives and mothers. The result, Wilson tells me, is that "while there've been more companies that offer flexibility, which helps, there's not a real commitment to making sure that there's a national child-care policy, that there are ways that women can enter and re-enter the workforce at the same level if they leave to have children, that there's complete support for paternity leave," which would allow men to share family responsibilities equally.

* * *

"Show me a woman without guilt, and I'll show you a man."—Marie C. Wilson

* * *

Wilson agrees that one of the things that keeps women out of positions of power is that "they're not just having to negotiate at work; women have to negotiate at home if they are in a two-career household, which they usually are." How do they get enough support at home to be able to do a 24/7 job? "I've often said, 'Show me a woman without guilt and I'll show you a man,'" she says. "Because frankly, women end up feeling guilty at work because they are not doing enough at home and feeling guilty at home because they're not doing enough at work."

My husband, Jim, is the son of a single mother who had to work and also struggled with mental-health issues. He had

no blueprint for "who does what" in the home. We negotiate our own path as a couple, and while it might not be perfect, it is not weighed down with traditional stereotypes.
Except for my year of unemployment, ours has always been
a two-career household. When the girls were babies, there
were several years where it could be argued that I carried a
heavier load at home, but my husband and I never counted.
Whoever was there did what needed to be done: we handled
the household duties and childcare in an equal partnership.
But these days, it's arguable that he contributes more than I
do. It just happened that way, without discussion. Family, to
us, is a collaboration, not an accounting of who's done what.
I feel so lucky that our marriage is based on mutual support;
the only thing we count is our blessings.

CONCLUSION

MY STORY
How It Ends—for Now

Over the past two decades, I've learned a great deal about what *not* to do when negotiating a raise, a job offer, or simply trying to push my career forward. I've benefited from my own experience, and the wealth of experience that the amazing women in this book were generous enough to share with me. I'm confident that I won't let myself down again. I am optimistic that it will be easier for generations to come, as it was easier for me than the generations that came before—just as long as we're able to transcend our fears and limitations, and be authentic and in the moment when it comes to negotiating for ourselves. Right now, our inability to do that is costing us money. We owe it to ourselves to do better.

Everyone I spoke with is optimistic about the future of women in the workforce. Even those who believe that men are holding us back also believe that at some point they will also lift us up. "I think we're making progress, and I think the best way to make progress is when more and more men have daughters," Valerie Jarrett tells me. She flourished in her career when she worked for Mayor Daley, whom she describes as a supportive father and a husband to a strong wife. She also points to President Obama, the son of a single mom, husband to a woman who has always had a demanding career, and concerned father of two girls. He surrounds himself with strong women, values them, and "lifts them up."

Many others felt the key was to have more women working in traditionally male fields. Not just traditional areas such as finance, but emerging fields like technology, which is increasingly a center of power.

"What's astonishing and quite disturbing is at the top of the capitalist pyramid there are almost no women," Chrystia Freeland says. "The areas where the real money and power reside are still occupied almost exclusively by men."

Freeland has covered the global economy for several decades as a reporter and editor of the *Financial Times*. Today she is the global editor-at-large for Reuters, and she often is on *Morning Joe* to talk about the world economy, business, and politics. While sitting with Freeland on our studio set one day, I mention my plans to write this book. She is instantly supportive: "Mika, women need to hear the truth."

That truth, says Freeland, is that when a job is high-status, society still defines it as male. "How many would picture a Wall Street titan in a skirt?" she asks. She sees the same thing developing in American science and technology industries right now.

"Most of the gain in income and productivity for the whole economy over the past decade, even the past couple of decades, is in the top one percent, and that's where the women aren't penetrating," Freeland says. "I want to see women coming up with something and creating it and building it. I want a female Sergey Brin, I want a female John Paulson. I think there are lots of women out there. We need to create a culture that encourages that more. Think about the great tech start-ups—think Apple, Microsoft, Google, Facebook. Where are the girls coming up with these great ideas in their Harvard dorm rooms?"

One reason for the lack of women in technology is that men with backgrounds in engineering, science, and math outnumber women four to one.

Studies by the Center for Women's Business Research reveal that even when women *do* come up with the ideas in their dorm rooms, they are not very likely to get the capital needed to create these kinds of high-growth start-ups.

But that's not the only reason women aren't flocking to these sectors. Sheryl Sandberg, COO of Facebook, has actually investigated why there aren't more women in the technology field. She points out that "the percentage of women getting computer science degrees is going down. And people with computer science degrees make a lot more money than people without; they get the right industries and the right jobs. One of the reasons, it turns out, is that boys play video games and girls don't. And people who play video games start coding, because they want to write things for their video games." Sandberg suggests that one of the steps we could take to get more women into computer science is to make more women-centric video games, and encourage little girls to play them.

This is counterintuitive advice. "I keep taking the computer away from my little girls," I say.

"Give it back," Sandberg says. "And when your daughters wonder why they get to play video games, tell them to thank me."

Yahoo CEO Carol Bartz agrees that educating our daughters will have an impact. "As parents, we let our daughters off the hook," she says. "I believe more women are needed in the ranks of all industries because we do have different perspectives. One of the things we look at at Yahoo is, how do people interface with technology? What do women look for versus what men look for versus what different age groups look for? For instance, we know that when women look to a screen, they look more to the left or right, men to the lower left, kids across the top." So the fact that designing a great user experience requires a combination of both technology and sociology should attract more women, she says, "because they actually believe they can add something more than just the raw algorithms, if you will."

Bartz continues, "I think women in general need to encourage our grade-school girls to stay with science and math so that they have an option. If their last big math course is sixth-grade algebra, they're never going to be an engineer.

Because by the time they think, 'Hey, I want to go into computer science,' guess what? There's no way to catch up."

Elizabeth Warren admits that she's more concerned than ever about women catching up. "You know, here's the funny part now. Because I'm older, I'm more experienced, right? I have a fancy chair at Harvard [and a special position at the White House], and I now find myself not furious on my own behalf, but furious on behalf of younger women, who fall into exactly the same traps I fell into."

But others, like the FDIC's Sheila Bair, are optimistic that things are changing: "I think one of the benefits of having women in senior positions is that we provide more models to younger women. They can see us sticking up for ourselves, taking credit for our ideas, demanding a seat at the table and an equal place to our male counterparts. I think being role models will help over time to change young women's attitudes about themselves."

How can we ensure that the next generation will have more female role models? Well, as I've said, we can only control what we can control. It's up to me to control my own behavior, to take responsibility for my own actions. Not wait to be acknowledged, but to step up and own my success. I've earned it.

Tina Brown points out that "Assuming power is everything. You have to assume it, and I don't think that women do. I think they wait to be asked." She gives an example from a breakfast she attended recently. Representative Nancy Pelosi was a speaker, and one of the women in the audience asked how we can stop men from dismissing our potential as leaders. "Nancy Pelosi said, 'You can't wait. You don't wait. I didn't ask anyone's permission to run. I just ran.' The answer is, the inmates have to seize the asylum. Ultimately, I think that the constant waiting for us to be part of the corporate power structure is not going to work—not going to happen. I think that's why they need to start their own companies."

I agree with Brown's approach: the way to shift the balance is not to try to change existing workplace dynamics but to take matters into your own hands. She continues: "If you're one woman in a room of seven men and the corporate structure is all male, you just feel you're not getting anywhere. And you either leave or you fight like hell or you're squashed. I think the best thing for women, frankly, when they find themselves in that situation, is to leave and start their own companies. I actually do think that women leading their own companies is where it's at. They will build different corporate structures and different networks, and that's going to be the healthy thing in the future."

Encouraging women to take control of their own destinies is very much at the heart of this book. That's why, when Valerie Jarrett asked me to moderate a panel at the recent Women's Entrepreneurship Conference, I couldn't say no, even though I was on deadline to finish this book.

The subject of the panel was Women-Owned Businesses in the 21st Century, and we were discussing the results of a recent report commissioned by the White House Council on Women and Girls about women entrepreneurs' access to capital. The report shows, for example, that women are not given loans as often as men; when they are, the loans are smaller, and although women start up as many businesses as men, they don't last.

On the day of the conference I rushed off the set of *Morning Joe*, barely made it to the White House, and got up on stage, breathless, in front of 200 women who run both small and large businesses.

My opening remarks were, "It's great to be here. I'm actually writing a book about knowing your value, and the results of this report are not only so important to us as women and where we're headed, but it's exactly what I've been writing about. We're making great strides, but we need to do better. In fact, it was Jarrett who, a year ago, sitting in her office, told me that I shouldn't just think about doing this book, that I *had* to do this book, and she inspired me to write it.

"And now a year later, by giving me the honor of being your moderator today, Jarrett has also inspired me to miss my deadline." The whole room exploded with laughter, and then I said, "But we're women. We'll get it done, right?" And they all started to cheer.

This book, like my memoir, *All Things at Once,* can't be wrapped up tidily at the end with a pretty bow. I don't pretend to have all the answers. I don't see myself featured on the cover of *Good Housekeeping* or *Fortune* magazine as the person who figured out how to have it all and do it all well. I've struggled in my public and private life to hit all the right notes, and I take full responsibility for my failings—as well as for my successes. And in terms of my earning what I'm worth, let's just say I'm getting there. I do know this: if I'd written this book ten years ago and taken the advice of its interviewees to heart, I'd be a multimillionaire today. Knowing the fair-market value of our contributions at work is a critically important piece of knowledge for today's (and tomorrow's) professional woman. Our families' future depends on our knowing what we should be paid, and getting it. If we can't quantify and communicate our value with confidence, the achievements of the tremendous women before us will have all been for nothing. Knowing our value and communicating it effectively is the next chapter in the story that began with the women's rights movement. Let's write it together, and let's get it done.

INDEX

Administrative Science Quarterly, 149
agents, 117–18
aggression, 61, 63, 78, 79–80, 87, 90, 135
All Things at Once (Brzezinski), 6, 185
Anderson, Cameron, 79
anger, 21, 49, 78, 88–89
apologies, 33, 84, 123–24, 129
Apple, 181
Apprentice, The (TV show), 60
assertiveness, 78–80, 85, 89, 92, 103
authenticity, 77–78
Autodesk, 44

Babcock, Linda, 40, 91
backlash effect, 78–80
Bair, Sheila, 7, 183
   and difficulty of getting people to listen, 107–8, 111–12
   emotionalism disdained by, 87–89
   on mentors, 145–46
   on motherhood, 159
   self-undervaluing by, 102–3
   subprime crisis and, 68, 107–8
   on Wall Street crisis, 67–70
Banfield, Ashleigh, 14
Bartz, Carol, 7
   on asking for raises, 124
   as assertive, 78
   compensation package of, 104–5
   on compliments, 90
   on confidence, 121, 122
   as confrontational, 112
   on education, 182–83
   on knowing salaries of peers, 119
   on quitting, 135
   self-undervaluing by, 44–45
   working mothers supported by, 174
Behar, Joy, 7, 80–82
   independence of, 136
behavioral economics, 66–67
Belkin, Lisa, 53
Benard, Stephen, 158
Bernanke, Ben, 146
bitches, ambitious women perceived as, 80, 81–82, 85, 161
body language, 123–24
Born, Brooksley, 7
   on being a working mother, 167–68
   on Wall Street crisis, 67–70, 108, 110–11
   on women helping women, 154–55
Bowles, Hannah Riley, 7
   on author's dispute with Griffin, 76, 78
   on diverse teams, 70
   flirting disdained by, 91
   on gender disparity in negotiating, 85–86

Bowles, Hannah Riley *(continued)*
  on gender disparity in network-
    ing, 76–77
  on raises, 126–27
  on role models, 93
  on sponsors, 146, 149–50
Brion, Sebastien, 79
British Columbia, University of, 58
Brown, Isabel, 169–70
Brown, Sarah, 153
Brown, Tina, 7
  on assuming power, 183–84
  female employee overlooked by,
    38–39
  institutionalized preference for
    men disdained by, 56–57
  on networking, 150
  on rejection, 134–35
  on working mothers, 169–70
Brzezinski, Ian, 22
Brzezinski, Mark, 23
Brzezinski, Mika:
  apologizing of, 33, 84
  in argument with manager,
    151–52
  book deal of, 144
  career moves of, 4
  clothes of, 26–27, 28, 126
  contract of, 19–20, 118, 144
  daughters of, 2, 12, 13, 17, 44,
    170, 178
  depression of, 30
  as desiring to be liked, 85
  expenses of, 2, 27, 28, 126
  financial problems of, 2, 21
  Griffin's dispute with, 28, 75–76,
    78, 85, 126, 143
  hair clip incident of, 83–85, 152
  Hillary Clinton's campaign
    covered by, 82–84
  marriage of, 177–78
  Morning Joe schedule of, 19–20,
    26–27
  negotiating skills of, 4

  as news reader, 12, 13
  news show offered to, 33–34, 50
  Paris Hilton incident and, 31–33,
    50, 152
  pay of, 2, 4–5, 27, 28, 144–45
  quitting considered by, 2
  radio show of, 144
  raise sought by, 1–5, 9, 27–29,
    55–56, 75–76, 78, 89, 115,
    126, 139–45, 151–52
  "relentlessly pleasant" behavior
    and, 91
  Scarborough's job offer to, 15–16
  self-undervaluing by, 4, 13,
    20–21, 22, 118, 140
  start at MSNBC, 11–12, 13–15
  start on *Morning Joe*, 17–18
  2008 election covered by, 1,
    22–26, 29, 82–84, 139, 157
Brzezinski, Zbigniew, 22–23,
    141–42
Bush, George W., 11, 68

Carter, Jimmy, 23
Catalyst, 54, 56, 57, 147
CBS Evening News, 3
CBS News, 11, 14, 144
Celebrity Roasts, 148
Center for Women's Business
    Research, 181
Child, 175
children, raising of, 8, 54, 157–78
Clinton, Bill, 23, 67, 90
Clinton, Hillary, 5, 82–84
CNBC, 101
collaboration, 63
Comedy Central, 148
Commodity Futures Trading Com-
    mission (CFTC), 67, 69, 111
compliments, 90
computer science, 182
Condé Nast, 134, 169
confidence, 41–43, 86, 113,
    121–22, 135–36

Congress, U.S., 117
Consumer Financial Protection
    Bureau, 98, 105
Correll, Shelley, 158
Cosmopolitan, 7, 96, 120, 131,
    175
credit card agreements, 109, 110
Curb Your Enthusiasm (TV show),
    65, 148–49

Daily Beast, 38, 123, 150, 169
Daley, Richard, 173, 180
David, Larry, 148–49
Deutsch, Donny, 7, 62–64, 66
    on aggressiveness, 63–64, 76,
        87
    on negotiations, 137–38
    on raises, 121, 124–25
Deutsche Telekom, 58
diversity, 70
Dobbins, Lucille, 36, 37
Dole, Elizabeth, 145–46
Dole, Robert, 145
double bind, 78–80
drive, 61

education, 51, 182–83
Effron, Mark, 173
election of 2008, 1, 22–26, 29,
    82–84, 139, 157
Elle, 39, 127, 166
Ely, Robin, 70
emotions, emotionalism, 45–47,
    88–89, 123, 133–34
entitlement, sense of, 96–102
Ephron, Nora, 7
    on favored nations, 127
    on quitting, 47–48, 136
    self-undervaluing by, 47–48
equal pay, *see* gender wage gap
Esquire, 48
Essman, Susie, 7, 64–65, 80–81
    on people skills, 90–91
    on sponsorship, 147–49

Facebook, 7, 41, 42, 44, 86, 162,
    176, 181
fear, 8, 35, 115, 121
Federal Deposit Insurance Corpo-
    ration (FDIC), 67–68, 69, 87,
    102, 107–8, 183
Financial Times, 180
flattery, 89–91
flirting, 91
Florio, Steve, 134–35
Flynn, Frank, 79, 80, 129–30
Forbes, 18, 87–88
Fortune 500, 44, 52
Freeland, Chrystia, 95, 180–81
Friars Club, 148

Gaston, Gina, 14
Geist, Willie, 3, 18, 20, 21, 29, 34,
    118
Geithner, Tim, 98
gender, *see* men; women
gender bias, subconscious, 54–57,
    79–80, 92
gender-neutrality, 59, 60
gender wage gap, 5, 6–7, 10, 39,
    40, 51–52, 53–54, 57–58, 70,
    117, 158
General Electric, 59, 77
"Getting a Job: Is There a Mother-
    hood Penalty?" (Correll,
    Benard, and Paik), 158
Glassdoor.com, 119
Google, 40, 181
Government Accountability Office
    (GAO), 52
Grand Hyatt Hotel, 61
Greenspan, Alan, 111
Griffin, Phil, 9–10, 19, 24, 25
    author's book project aided by,
        9–10
    author's dispute with, 28, 75–76,
        78, 85, 126, 143
    Scarborough's arguments with,
        73–75, 76

group-think, 68
guilt, 165, 177

hair clip incident, 83–85, 152
Harvard University, 55
Hegewisch, Ariane, 54
Herbert, Joe, 66–67
Hoffer, Jim, 13, 177–78
HomePage, 14
housework, 54, 176, 178
Houston, University of, 98
Huffington, Arianna, 7, 96
  on asking for raises, 48–49
  on fear, 121
  on stereotypes of outspoken
    women, 92–93
  on women supporting women,
    153
Huffington Post, 49, 92, 96
Hush (White), 96–97

Ibarra, Herminia, 77
Imus, Don, 14, 15, 17, 19, 141
Institute for Women's Policy
  Research, 54
Iowa, 23–25
Iraq War, 31

Jack, 96–97
Jarrett, Valerie, 35–38, 180, 184,
  185
  author aided by, 6–7
  on being a working mother,
    168–69
  on good bosses, 173–74
  on negotiation, 104, 128
  on rejection, 132–33
Joint Economics Committee,
  158

Karan, Donna, 153
King, Alan, 148
Kray, Laura, 91

Lang, Ilene H., 54, 56, 57, 58, 64
Licht, Chris, 18, 23–24, 76
likeability, success vs., 86–87
Lilly Ledbetter Fair Pay Act, 6
loans, 184–85
luck, 41, 45, 50

McCain, John, 22, 81
McCaskill, Claire, 65–66
  on motherhood, 159–61
Mademoiselle, 175
Maloney, Carolyn B., 158
"man-cession," 10
marriage, 9, 176–78
MBAs, 51, 57, 79–80
Meet the Press, 25
men:
  confidence of, 41, 42–43, 113
  emotions and, 47
  institutionalized preference for,
    55–57
  as more connected to senior
    executives than women, 77
  networking by, 76–77, 150
  overestimating performance by,
    41, 54, 55
  peers' salaries known to, 118,
    119
  raises and, 123, 124, 129–30
  rejection accepted by, 132
  score-keeping by, 103
  women's imitation of, 77–78
mentors, 38, 145–47, 153
Michigan, 25
Microsoft, 181
modesty, 86–87
More, 45, 119, 125, 162
Morning Joe, 1–5, 7, 38, 144, 180,
  185
  author's desire to quit, 1–2
  author's schedule at, 19–20
  author's start with, 15–18, 118
  hair clip incident on, 83–85, 152

Hillary Clinton's campaign covered by, 83–84
on-air chemistry of, 3, 15–16, 31, 32
Paris Hilton incident on, 31–33, 50, 152
2008 election covered by, 1, 22–26, 29
motherhood, mothers, 157–78
four-day workweeks of, 166
pay gap of, 158
self-undervaluing by, 164–65, 166, 169
value added by, 163–64, 165, 167–69
value decreased by, 161–63
MSNBC, 2, 19, 20, 24–25, 28
author given raise by, 1–5, 9, 27–29, 55–56, 75–76, 78, 89, 115, 126, 139–44, 151–52
author's start at, 11–12, 13–15
financial restructuring of, 3
research for book done by, 10, 34–35
salaries at, 116–17

National Equal Pay Day, 6
NBC, 12, 13–14, 59, 83
NBC News, 12, 25
NBC News Special Report, 14
NBC Nightly News, 20, 83
negotiations, 104
confidence in, 135–36
gender gap in, 70, 85–86, 91–92, 146
ineffective techniques of, 4
power vs. fear in, 8, 115
rejection in, 132–34
see also raises, negotiating
networking skills, 76–77, 79, 147–50, 154
New Hampshire, 25, 82–84
Newsweek, 38, 123

New Yorker, 18, 134
New York Magazine, 48, 67, 76
New York Times, 18, 142
New York Times Magazine, 53
Norway, 58
Nosek, Brian, 55–56

Obama, Barack, 6, 22, 23, 35, 173, 180
Obama, Michelle, 174
Obama, Sasha, 174
O'Connor, Sandra Day, 145
O'Donnell, Grace, 172
O'Donnell, Henry, 171–72
O'Donnell, Lawrence, 66
O'Donnell, Norah, 164–65, 171–72
O'Donnell, Riley, 171–72
opinion television, 19
optimism, 179–80
"opt-out revolution," 176–77
Orman, Suze, 7, 49
on financial safety nets, 136–37
on raises, 115–16, 127, 130, 137
sense of entitlement of, 101–2

Paik, In, 158
Paris Hilton incident, 31–33, 50, 152
passive-aggressive tactics, 112
Paul, Ron, 23
Paulson, Hank, 108
Paycheck Fairness Act, 6, 117
Payscale.com, 119
Pelosi, Nancy, 183–84
people skills, 90–91
pregnancy, 171–73
Project Implicit, 55
promotions, requesting, 38
gender gap in, 8, 34–35, 40, 64, 122–23, 158
self-promotion and, 35–38

Quindlen, Anna, 92
quitting, 47–48, 134–38

raises, negotiating, 8, 49
  achievements and, 115–16, 120
  author's problem with, 1–5, 9,
    27–29, 55–56, 75–76, 78, 89,
    115, 126, 139–45, 151–52
  confidence and, 122, 135–36
  "favored-nations" argument
    and, 127–28
  fear in, 35, 115
  gender gap in, 34–35, 40, 47,
    123, 124, 129–30
  market value and, 116–19, 120
  men's detachment from, 123,
    124, 129–30
  mistakes in asking for, 122–25,
    179
  Orman's advice on, 115–16, 127,
    130, 137
  relational account and, 85–86
  strategies in asking for, 85,
    115–22
  timing and, 120
Ratigan, Dylan, 66
rejection, 22, 132–38
relational account, 85–86
relationships, 8
  see also marriage
resumes, 54–55
Reuters, 95, 180
Rhode, Deborah, 52
risk taking, 68
Roizen, Heidi, 79
role models, 93, 183
Rubin, Robert, 111
Russert, Tim, 25, 172, 173
Rutgers University, 14

salaries, 5
  gender gap in, 5, 6–7, 10, 39,
    51–52, 53–54, 57–58, 70, 117,
    158

  information on ranges of,
    116–19
  personal attributes and, 149
Salary.com, 119
Sandberg, Sheryl, 7, 40–44, 45,
    86–87
  on marriage, 176
  modesty of, 86–87
  on motherhood, 162–63
  raise requested by, 43–44
  self-undervaluing by, 43–44, 45
  on women in technology,
    181–82
Scarborough, Joe:
  author offered job by, 15–16
  author's raise and, 1–5, 139–44
  Griffin's arguments with, 73–75,
    76
  Hillary Clinton's capmaign cam-
    paign covered by, 82–83, 84
  pay of, 2–3, 5, 29, 141, 151
  rebelliousness of, 21–22
Scarborough, Susan, 141
Scarborough Country, 15
Schwarzenegger, Arnold, 108
science, 180
self-promotion, 35–38, 39–40,
    44–45, 102–6
Senate, U.S., 117, 160
Seymour, Lesley Jane, 7, 119, 125,
    130–31
  on contracts, 151
  emotions disdained by, 45–47
  on motherhood, 162
  on negotiations, 130–31
  self-undervaluing by, 46
Sher, Susan, 173–74
60 Minutes, 11, 12, 29
Smith, Carol, 39, 127
  on emotions, 133–34
  on hiring mothers, 165–66
  on rejection, 133–34
social capital, 149
South Carolina, 25

sponsorship, 146–50
stereotyping, 91, 92–93
Stiller, Jerry, 148
subconscious biases, 54–57, 79–80, 92, 102
subprime mortgage crisis, 68, 107–10
success, likeability vs., 86
Supreme Court, U.S., 51, 53

Take Our Daughters and Sons to Work Day®, 52
TARP, 105
technology, 180, 181–82
thirty-three percent, as magic number, 53, 92
Thomas, David, 70
Thomas, Marlo, 92
Time, 98
Time Warner, 39
Treasury Department, U.S., 40
Trump, Donald, 7, 59, 60–62
  on aggression, 135
  on motherhood, 161–62
Trump Tower, 60–61

undervaluing of self, 4, 5
  by author, 4, 13, 20–21, 22, 118, 140
  by Bair, 102–3
  by Bartz, 44–45
  by Ephron, 47–48
  by mothers, 164–65, 166, 169
  by Sandberg, 43–44, 45
  by Seymour, 46

value, 4–10
  aggression and, 61, 63, 78, 79–80, 87, 90, 135
  confidence and, 41–43, 86, 113, 121–22, 135–36
  downplaying self and, 86–87
  emotions and, 45–47, 88–89, 123, 133–34

and overlooking of women, 38–39
people skills and, 90–91
self-promotion and, 35–38, 39–40, 44–45, 105–6
subconscious biases and, 54–57, 79–80, 92, 102
and taking oneself seriously, 47–48
and wanting to be liked, 80–82, 85
see also promotions, requesting; raises, negotiating; undervaluing of self
Vanity Fair, 169–70
Vault.com, 119
video games, 181–82
View, The (TV show), 81, 136
Virginia, University of, 55

Wall Street, 107
Wall Street Journal, 106, 133
Wall Street meltdown, 66–70, 88, 105–6
Warren, Elizabeth, 7, 108, 183
  on making oneself heard, 109–10, 112
  "self-promotion" by, 105–6
  on sense of entitlement, 97–100
Washington, University of, 55
Washington Post, 67
Weekend Today, 20
Welch, Jack, 7, 59–60, 62, 77
  on confidence, 135–36
  on women being heard, 112–13
WFSB Channel 3, 173
Wharton School of Finance, 61
White, Hunter, 175
White, Kate, 7, 96–97
  on being pressured in negotiations, 131–32
  on raises, 120, 128–29
White House Council on Women and Girls, 6, 184

White House Project, 52
*Why Good Girls Don't Get Ahead
    but Gutsy Girls Do* (White), 96
Williams, Brian, 14
Wilson, Marie C., 52–53, 91–92
  on opt-out revolution, 176–77
  on women's connections, 147
women:
  aggressiveness and, 63, 78,
    79–80, 87, 90, 135
  as allegedly harder workers,
    59–61
  as allegedly more collaborative,
    62
  anger and, 21, 49, 78, 88–89
  and arguments with superiors, 74
  assertiveness of, 78–80, 85, 89,
    92, 103
  better people skills of, 90–91
  bottom line aided by, 58–59
  as caregivers, 53–54
  as CEOs, 44, 52–53
  challenges faced by, 7–8
  connection to senior executives,
    77
  as good for business, 58–71
  as hard on other women,
    151–55
  lack of confidence of, 42–43, 86,
    113, 121–22
  large salaries earned by, 5
  making self heard, 106–13
  men imitated by, 77–78
  mistakes in asking for raises,
    122–25
  networking by, 77, 147–50, 154
  overlooking of, 38–39
  peers' salaries not known to,
    118–19

  perceived as bitches, 80, 81–82,
    85, 161
  promotions requested by, 8,
    34–35, 38, 64, 122–23, 158
  raises requested by, *see* raises,
    negotiating
  rejection and, 132–33
  relationship to money, 49
  role models for, 93, 183
  score-keeping by, 103
  self-promotion by, 102–6
  self-undervaluing by, 4, 6, 7, 8,
    44–45, 47, 102–3, 127–28, 164
  sense of entitlement lacking in,
    96–102
  as stand-up comedians, 65
  in technology fields, 180, 181–82
  underestimating performance
    by, 41, 54, 55
  wage gap of, 5, 6–7, 10, 39,
    51–52, 53–54, 57–58, 70, 117,
    158
  see also motherhood, mothers
*Women & Money: Owning the Power
    to Control Your Destiny*
    (Orman), 116
Women Don't Ask (Babcock), 40
Women: Inspiration & Enterprise
    Symposium, 153
Women-Owned Business in the
    21st Century, 184–85
Women's Bar Association, 154
Women's Entrepreneurship Con-
    ference, 184–85
Working Woman, 96–97, 131
work-life balance, 6, 157–58

Yahoo, 7, 44, 78, 90, 104, 124, 174,
    182